# Friends Forever

# Friends Forever

## William L. Coleman

**BETHANY HOUSE PUBLISHERS**
MINNEAPOLIS, MINNESOTA 55438
A Division of Bethany Fellowship, Inc.

Photos by Dick Easterday with special thanks to the Action For Teens
group of Bethany Missionary Church.

All scripture quotations in this publication are from the Holy Bible, New
International Version. Copyright © 1973, 1978, International Bible Society. Used by permission of Zondervan Bible Publishers.

Published by Bethany House Publishers
A Division of Bethany Fellowship, Inc.
6820 Auto Club Road, Minneapolis, Minnesota 55438

Printed in the United States of America

**Library of Congress Cataloging-in-Publication Data**

Coleman, William L.
    Friends forever.

    1. Youth—Prayer-books and devotions—English.
2. Friendship—Religious aspects—Christianity.
I. Title.
BV4850.C5648    1987        241'.676        87–700
ISBN 0–87123–959–0 (pbk.)

June Coleman has worked extensively on the volume, helping select subjects and reading the final draft. I appreciated both her discussions and encouragement.

# About the Author

WILLIAM L. COLEMAN is the well-known author of nearly three dozen books on a wide variety of topics. Combining his vast experience as a pastor, researcher, writer and speaker, Bill is noted for his effective devotional writing in the area of family relationships. He has been married for over twenty years and is the father of three children.

## Other Teen Devotionals
## from Bethany House Publishers

# Table of Contents

# Friends Forever

# *Give Us People!*

The Grand Canyon is breathtaking. Thousand-foot waterfalls are beautiful. Computers are intriguing. But none are as exciting as people.

People sing in parks at midnight, eat pig-out sundaes and slide down snowbanks on their stomachs. People put fish in your locker, study history half the night and sit beside you when you break up with your steady. When the bands stop playing, the lights go out and you leave school for the last time, it's the friends that you remember.

Friends are too important to take lightly. They deserve the right attention and some generous sharing. This book is aimed at keeping friendships alive and rewarding, just the way God invented them.

Bill Coleman
Aurora, Nebraska

# Even Good Friends Can Sit on Your Lunch

Charlie loved to smash lunches. You didn't dare leave your sack lunch around or Charlie would grab it and throw it against the wall as hard as he could. Everyone laughed, so you did too. As you pulled out your flat cupcake, your crumpled potato chips and your twisted baloney sandwich, you gave it your best smile.

If sack-lunch throwing began to bore Charlie, he had a second trick. Charlie would seize any unprotected lunch bag and sit on it. One good flop and the poor victim's chocolate chips were never the same.

Lunch-mashing wasn't Charlie's most outstanding characteristic, however. When most people thought of Charlie, they remembered the fact that he was a good friend. And it's all right for a good friend to sit on your lunch once in a while.

Even our best friends will do dumb things from time to time. They tell secrets when they shouldn't. They lose your gold necklace or make a snide remark about your clothes, and it hurts.

You laugh it off because you don't want to seem like a rag. But they have cut you deeply. It may not be crucial if someone sits on your lunch, but who really wants to eat smashed Twinkies?

That's part of the price friends pay for friendship. If we are willing to get close to others, we have to take chances. If we are to enjoy the company of the people we like, we risk getting bruised. But we know it's worth it because good friends are important.

Naturally, if friends hurt too much, if they cut too deeply, the relationship won't work. Some teenagers and adults keep friendships going even though their friends are abusing them. That's a sick relationship that needs to end.

Everyone sits on your lunch once in a while. But if that friend sits on your lunch every day, maybe you need to look for a safer friend.

Of course any "joke" done maliciously from spite or revenge is no laughing matter. Though the joke may seem harmless enough, if it causes hurt or damage, it is sin, not a joke.

When good friends get "out of hand" or go too far, their actions should remind us to look at ourselves. How often do we push our friends too far? How often do we take unfair advantage of a solid friendship?

It's all right to sit on someone's lunch sometimes. But only fools sit on lunches all the time.

We learn to forgive our friends when they do strange things. Hopefully, they are able to forgive us, too.

*"Forgive, and you will be forgiven"* (Luke 6:37).

## Some things to think about:

1. Do you have a friend who does absurd things? Why do you like him?
2. What are the keys to forgiveness?

# *Friends Forever*

That's another thing about having Christian friends—you can have them forever.

You may change locations and move thousands of miles away. But you will get together again someday. You may find different interests and drift apart. But that won't matter either. Years from now you can meet again and share plenty of interests.

Christians become separated, but only for a while. In the "forever" they are reunited because they belong to Jesus Christ.

The Bible doesn't tell us what we will be doing "forever." Will we cruise around on clouds? It's hard to picture ourselves sitting on the running boards of chariots at Gabriel's Drive-in, but how do you really know? Can you imagine electric harps or angels rapping? It all boggles the mind.

No, the Bible doesn't say any of that. In fact, it doesn't fill in many details. The bare essentials are these: Jesus Christ will be there and we will all bow our knees to Him (Phil. 2:10). Jesus will be the number-one attraction.

We also know we will be changed in the great "forever." That probably means no more frizzy hair, no more braces, and most of us will be down to one chin. All of that is speculation, but we assume that changes will be improvements.

The third thing we know is that Christian friends will get together. It's the great class reunion, and we won't want to miss it.

"Forever" is a special gift that God gives to believers. It allows us to make friends in history class and keep them for longer than we can count.

*"Dear friends, now we are children of God, and what we will be has not yet been made known. But we know that when he appears, we shall be like him, for we shall see him as he is"* (1 John 3:2).

## Some things to think about:

1. Have you had a Christian friend move away? Was that separation easier because you are Christians?
2. Do you feel that your Christian friends are spiritual brothers and sisters?

# *Best Friends*

"I feel guilty wanting to be with one person most of the time, but I really do like Brenda. What's wrong with having a best friend?"

There isn't anything wrong with having a best friend, and there is no need to feel guilty. People are naturally drawn more to one person than others. Normally we don't plan to create a best friend; it simply happens. However, there are some difficulties that go with the territory.

If our relationship becomes too exclusive, we may suffer some consequences. There are built-in headaches. For one thing, having just one friend tends to smother our friendship and will probably shorten its life. Maintained at a measured pace, friendships can last for years, even decades. If your friends are given breathing room, they are more likely to enjoy the freedom of your relationship.

When two friends are bound too tightly, they also have a tendency to frighten everyone else off. It's unwise to become isolated from a wider circle of companions. This may not happen often, but when it does everyone is prevented from getting to know good people.

Most of us realize that we can't be everyone's best friend. However, it's possible for two or three to tie into the best-friend category. Generally we are happy to be part of that wider circle and are content to be a steady friend.

Friendships are important enough to evaluate from time to time. Where is your friendship heading? Are you being a considerate friend? Do you try to do what your friend enjoys or are you beginning to insist on your own way too much? How often do you do something extra for your friend simply because he is your friend?

While some best friends tend to stay around for many years, most do not. You have probably changed best friends several times and likely will again. People change and they change at different rates. It's hard to keep our relationships the same.

A look at Jesus Christ finds that He had several interesting friendships. He had many acquaintances and a large

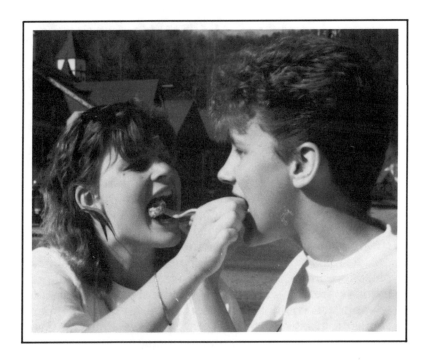

circle of friends. There was also a group of twelve who had a special relationship with Him.

Three of those twelve could be described as extra close friends. They were James, John and Peter. From that trio one friend seems to stand out. He called himself the "disciple whom Jesus loved." That person was probably John.

Best friends make up a closeness that is perfectly normal. They need to be handled with love, but they are well worth the added attention.

*"One of them, the disciple whom Jesus loved, was reclining next to him"* (John 13:23).

## Some things to think about:

1. Tell why you enjoy being with your best friend.
2. Do you know friendships that are so tight there is no room to breathe?
3. Do your best friend and you try to reach out to become friends with others?

# Few Quarterbacks and Cheerleaders

Some of the greatest people you can meet are quarterbacks or cheerleaders. The opposite is also true. There are a number of genuine jerks who have held those positions. They have been mean, snobbish—even cruel. *Jerk* isn't too strong a word for some of them.

The roles we play in life have never made us good people. More important than what we do is the question of who we are. It's too bad that many of us mope around wishing we could become someone else. Contentment comes from making peace with ourselves and with God. No one has ever become a better person because he was selected for a team or named Roach Queen.

Value comes from inside, placed there by God. Others cannot give it to us or take it away.

If you want to be a cheerleader or a quarterback, give it a shot. It could be exciting. But if you are turned down, don't feel like ear wax. The significant things in life come from the inside; they are never placed on us from the outside.

Mary received an award from the local Optimist Club. They named her an outstanding youth. At the luncheon the presenter said, "Many of us want our children to grow up to become doctors or lawyers, but most important we want them to grow up to become good people. This award is presented today because Mary is a good person."

Try out for whatever you think you might enjoy. But don't get carried away by the supposed glamor. If you are rejected from that role, life goes on, and often goes on better. Most people who are turned down discover more satisfaction later than they could have imagined. They learned something about the true values of life.

If you learn that while you are a teenager, thank God. Too often we don't understand that until we are at least fifty years old.

Jesus liked to be accepted. He knew it was best for everyone involved. Yet, He realized that rejection was also part of His ministry. It hurt Him to be turned down, but He knew that popularity wasn't the great goal of life. Living out His life in harmony with His Father was the most important thing.

## Some things to think about:

1. Which means more to you: being popular or being content with who you are?
2. Do you know teens who have an obsession with receiving honors? Tell about it.

# *Parent-Teen*
# *Dialogue*

How many parents and teenagers do you know who have written each other off? Neither of them believes the other has anything worth saying. They have stopped talking, listening and sharing.

The stalemate is complicated because each thinks the other is the problem. If asked, they would point the finger and say, "He/she won't listen." They probably won't make much progress until each sees himself as the logjam and decides to break loose.

That puts communication squarely on your shoulders—whoever you might be. We must take the responsibility to thoughtfully open the dialogue. Those who make the attempt reap a truckful of practical help.

Begin to carve out a setting where you and a parent could talk. There are several steps that will make it easier.

1. Find a time when the parent is most likely to be in a decent mood. Just after work is miserable; right after supper could be a winner.

2. Turn off the television. Make sure the program on it isn't the news (many parents center their lives on the elections in Zaire). Ask if it's all right as you punch the knob to off.

3. Have one or two questions ready. Don't begin by lecturing your parents or being argumentative. Like everyone else, parents are flattered if someone will ask their opinions.

4. Plan to talk for just ten minutes. Don't make it a burden for anyone. By making it a pleasant experience for both of you, you will build bridges that allow more time later.

5. Hold your strong opinion until later. Convince your parent that you are not *just* interested in straightening out his ideas. When he finds you a good listener, he is more likely to eventually listen to you.

Parents feel better about young people who seek out their wisdom. They know the teenagers are at least willing to listen.

Ideally, parents would take the same easy steps to open a conversation with you; however, there is little that is ideal in life.

Remember, parents do have a wide variety of excellent experience. If we drop our barriers and talk more openly, we could save ourselves a tremendous amount of friction.

*"Listen, my sons, to a father's instruction; pay attention and gain understanding"*(Prov. 4:1).

## Some things to think about:

1. Do you know someone who has great difficulty in talking? Explain.
2. When is a good time to have discussions at your house?
3. List some ideas that make a discussion go better.

# Dull Churches

If you and your friends attend a church where the service is interesting, the sermons are helpful and you are worshiping God, take your minister out for a double taco special. Some teenagers find their church a satisfying place on most Sundays. However, too many find the pew experience about as fascinating as a lecture on letter-folding.

There is no doubt that church can be dull as a brick. But sometimes it isn't the church's fault. It could be that we aren't giving it a fair shot. Before blaming the deacons, we need to ask how we can help.

The answer doesn't lie in bringing gerbils to church or asking the choir to sing a selection of Tina Turner tunes. Even the suggestion of serving pizza during the offering could get your membership suspended.

For those willing to try, here are a few improvements we could make.

1. *Cut out the Late, Late Early Bird Theatre.* After watching Monsoon Mike Eats Manila until 3:00 a.m., it's hard to be alert during a church service. If we treated school this way, we would flunk.

2. *Take a piece of paper and a pencil.* If we jot down a couple of notes, we might find our gray cells much more willing to cooperate.

3. *Ask God to help you through the service.* If we expect something, we are far more likely to receive it. It's hard for God to steer us once we decide to put our lives in park.

4. *Drop a note to the minister.* Most pastors would love to know what teenagers consider important and relevant. Give him some idea of what you feel would be a helpful sermon for you and your friends. I bet you will soon hear the subject discussed from the pulpit.

5. *Make friends at the church.* It's difficult to feel like you are part of the service if you are a pew bug. Get to know the other young people, and your interest may rocket to the top.

God has big plans for the church and for you. Hopefully those plans include the two of you together. You can't afford to sit back and ask the church to entertain. Take charge of your own life and make the Sunday service part of it.

We need Christian friends and they need us. By keeping the church alive, we can come together and help each other.

*"Let us not give up meeting together, as some are in the habit of doing, but let us encourage one another—and all the more as you see the Day approaching"* (Heb. 10:25).

## Some things to think about:

1. Tell your favorite parts of a church service.
2. What topics would you like discussed in church?
3. What activities at church are your favorites?

# Change Is Tough

Why are there books about teenagers? You don't see many bestsellers on how to survive age twenty-five or how to handle relationships at seventy-nine. What is so unusual about ages thirteen through nineteen to warrant this much attention?

The fact is, the teen years are unique because of one word: change. Rapid, uneven, unpredictable change. We change at other ages also, but never as dramatically as in junior high and senior high.

Change can be painful. Even good change hurts because we leave one safe place for another. With teenagers change is happening all the time.

Their new height, voice, bone structure and shoe size are only part of the story. Teenagers are adjusting their relationships to their parents almost weekly. Their status in society is lunging forward; they race from a ten-speed to a '62 Chevy almost overnight. Yesterday's boys were pests, sticking rubber bugs down their friends' backs. Today they are square shouldered hall-dwellers with combs in their pockets. During their senior year in high school they become old enough to be drafted and go off to war.

Yesterday they were tempted to put half-eaten sandwiches on the teacher's chair. Today they are led away by booze and the offer of pot.

Too much change too fast. Maybe the teen years are too long. There are three thousand nights between the beginning of puberty and the time the average person gets married. Change comes quickly and slowly at the same time.

"Act your age" doesn't mean much in a confusing world. Are you a kid, an adult, an adolescent—or none of the above? It's bewildering. And teenagers can feel it.

That's why there are few easy answers. Most adults are as stumped as the young people themselves.

Smart teenagers are trying to let go of childhood and take hold of adulthood very carefully. One block at a time.

The foolish ones bring their childhood with them. The brash ones believe they are adults overnight and take on too much. Often they get knocked around because they are not yet ready for the responsibility that goes along with being an adult.

The adjustment of becoming an adult can go smoothly if you take one step at a time, moving steadily ahead at an even pace. Not rushing ahead and not dragging your heels makes the change seem much less drastic.

*"When I was a child, I talked like a child, I thought like a child, I reasoned like a child. When I became a man, I put childish ways behind me"* (1 Cor. 13:11).

## Some things to think about:

1. Tell about a friend or older brother or sister who grew into adulthood smoothly.
2. List some guidelines for moving into adulthood smoothly.

# Insulted

The police had arrested a man who killed two people with a shotgun. There was nothing mean about his appearance; he was polite, almost shy. As they recorded all of the details, they asked him why he did it. His answer was: "They called me names."

It seemed simple to him. The people had insulted him and he had to get them for it. Often, people mangle each other because they can't handle insults.

Calling people names is part of our dark culture. We hear it everywhere—at ball games, in the hall, in homes. How often has someone in a car driven past and yelled out an ugly name? And he doesn't even know you!

Insults are at the core of our society. Smart people learn how to handle them while they are young. If we spend our time boiling over because of name-calling, we will be steamed a great deal of the time.

First of all, divide the insults. Some are actually friendly. They may hurt, but the person who hurled them meant no harm. In fact, he probably was trying to say he liked you. It's a strange form of compliment, but many of us use it.

Some insults are one shot and it's over. The person was being cruel but it probably won't happen again. Chalk it up to the evil people do, then go on with life. It hurts, but throw it off before the insult starts to warp your attitude. In fact, *praying* for the person who hurt you is not only obeying Jesus, it also prevents you from becoming bitter.

Often people we know insult us without realizing what they are saying. If they keep it up, you might want to kindly tell them it bothers you. They probably never intended to hurt you and will quit the minute you mention it. This usually works best with friends.

Whatever approach we take, one reaction is strictly bad news. It's never smart to try to get even. To insult back only intensifies the problem. To try to get even only invites tremendous pain.

Jesus taught us a solid principle about insults. If someone hits us on one cheek, we are to turn the other cheek toward him. We don't fight back and we don't get even. We might ignore the insult or we might correct the person, but it's nutty to try to get even.

The younger we are when we grab hold of that principle, the smoother life will go for us.

*"But I tell you, Do not resist an evil person. If someone strikes you on the right cheek, turn to him the other also"* (Matt. 5:39).

## Some things to think about:

1. What is your first reaction when you're insulted?
2. Do you insult others, even in fun? If so, do you think you should change?
3. What is the best way to react to insults?

# *Helping Other Teens*

At a high school in the Midwest a group of teenagers banded together to help other teens. They saw a terrible problem: those in their own age group had troubles and were reluctant to talk to parents or teachers. However, a large number of teenagers are willing to discuss their headaches with peers.

Soon, one hundred-fifty young people organized themselves in the local school of one thousand students. They discovered that many teenagers had some kind of difficulty with drinking, sex, grades, parents, boyfriends, girlfriends, teachers or related subjects.

This group of young people decided to show other students that they cared and, when possible, to recommend solutions. If they felt the dilemma was too serious, the teenagers would suggest places where they could get other help.

Eventually the group won the International Youth Year Award presented by the U.S. Department of Education.

Teenagers aren't the wild, unruly bunch they are frequently made out to be. Many are thoughtful, helpful people in a world where it sounds corny to be that way.

This group chose to address a need where other young people seemed willing to respond. The great majority of teenagers indicate that when they face a crisis, they are more likely to talk to another young person than to an adult. That gives teenagers a terrific opportunity to help others and to find help themselves.

Of course it is possible to get bad advice from a friend, but that usually is not the case. The voice of experience beats going it alone. Going solo during a time of extreme pressure is one of the least productive things people can do.

Besides, most of us are not looking for advice. We may need nothing more than a good listener. By hearing ourselves explain our problem out loud, we may find our own solution.

People are essential—especially in tough times. Christian young people have excellent potential for getting close to other teenagers when they're in the dumper. A sympathetic ear and a knowledge that someone cares are potent medicines when we need them. When it's called for, a well-chosen suggestion or two can make all the difference.

If the person isn't a Christian, and the time is right, you could tell him about the ultimate Counselor, Jesus Christ.

*"You guide me with your counsel, and afterward you will take me into glory"* (Ps. 73:24).

## Some things to think about:

1. Whom have you found to be a good listener?
2. Do you go to your pastor for counseling?

# Boring Friends

Recently I heard a group that is making a study of the behavior of boring people. Their conclusions aren't final, but so far the study points toward this: those who continually complain about how tough they have it are boring. If we stop to think of the friends we know, this probably isn't too surprising. If we're smart, we will also take inventory of ourselves. We might be driving our friends nuts.

Every one of us has problems. That's part of the human condition. From time to time we need to lay our problems out to a friend. That's the nature of friendship. We need to lean on each other when the going gets tough. By sharing our hurts with someone else, a little of our pain goes away. None of us should give that up.

The "bores" are the ones who are problem-centered. They move from agony to agony, seldom coming up for air. If you see them coming, you can predict their mood and attitude. It's going to be the pits!

We soon begin to avoid them, much as we would a miserable situation. Why? Because when we feel up and happy, they will begin to drag us down. When we are already in a blue funk, they may torpedo us altogether.

A famous football coach recently said, "Life is played with pain." That's true for all of us. Some of that disappointment must be borne by ourselves. It makes us stronger and better able to cope. But when it becomes too much, we have to siphon it off on our friends.

It's the person who gripes daily that sends your brain waves screaming. They complain about teachers, parents, mailmen, boyfriends, newspaper print and chicken inspectors. And worse yet, it is all happening to them. Poor miserable, unappreciated suffering folk!

The constant complainers are first cousins to the talkathon friends. They consider their opinions the most important in the known world, and give their opinions relentlessly. Rattling on every minute, they have no patience to listen to anyone else.

If we talk all the time, we make our friends feel useless. They begin to wonder if their views are even worth anything. After a while these friends begin to feel unimportant in our presence and soon may stay away.

Good friends aren't afraid to talk about the things that genuinely bother them. But they keep it under control. They don't want to become like a toothache that irritates and never goes away.

They are also glad to share their opinions. However, they don't drown out their friends. At the core of every friendship, we are saying we value that person's views.

*"A fool finds no pleasure in understanding but delights in airing his own opinions"* (Prov. 18:2).

## Some things to think about:

1. Do you have fun friends?
2. Are you a fun friend? Explain.
3. List some guidelines to being a fun person.

# *Friends Who Hurt Us*

Toni said she would be there Saturday morning to help, but it soon became apparent she wasn't going to show up. Sharon spent the morning putting up decorations for the party and thinking about Toni. Each time she taped a streamer or blew up a balloon, she became more upset with her friend.

Not that Toni wasn't a good person—they had many laughs together. But Toni had a poor memory and she wasn't always considerate of others. That really ticked Sharon.

Every friend has a few quirks. He may do many things well, but have a couple of weaknesses that stand out. Close friends have learned to tolerate each other because they have so much to offer. If we have a friend who is doing something that especially annoys us, we do have some options. First, we can just ignore the offense. Some irritations come with the territory. We can't let every problem tear up our relationship. If it's only occasional and not too severe, let it ride. Blurting out at each ripple will only lead to hurt feelings.

The Bible puts it this way, "He who covers over an offense promotes love" (Prov. 17:9).

Good friendships deserve a generous tolerance. That will prove true on the job, with a spouse, or any other relationship we develop.

A second possibility is to confront your friend over the tension he is creating. We do this if the problem is repeated and hurting us too much. Gentle confrontation need not be ugly. And it's much better than losing a solid relationship that we might have saved.

If you have a strong friendship, it will weather one or two tactful corrections. When you do it carefully and lovingly, you can help the person and save your relationship.

No one enjoys being criticized. We pretend it's a great thing, but criticism is a powerful ego-crusher and should never be used lightly. That's why we cover over our pain when we can. However, if we cover up too much, we end up with piles of garbage that can't be seen but are definitely there.

Friends sometimes hurt us. That is part of being with people. Patient friends overlook what they can and learn to deal with what they find difficult to tolerate. This way they maintain some friends for many years.

## Some things to think about:

1. Have you confronted a friend about something he does that bothers you?
   What happened?
2. Have you dropped a friend because he was careless about your feelings?
3. Has a friend criticized you? Did it help?

# The Kidnapping

When they came to get June, she was sitting on the couch in her living room, wearing sweatpants and no makeup. Her hair looked like seaweed, and she certainly wasn't expecting company, let alone a kidnapping.

Christie and Kelly tried to talk her into walking to the car peacefully, but June wouldn't hear of it. Left with no choice, they tussled with her and finally, with the help of June's father, carried her, kicking and screaming, to the car. Naturally the neighbors stopped what they were doing, children pulled up on their bikes—even dogs and cats hurried over.

There aren't many kidnappings in June's community. This one became the social highlight of the week.

It was a clever way to celebrate June's birthday without getting too sentimental or mushy. This was a safe way for friends to tell each other how much they cared.

Life is serious too much and too long. It needs a fine balance of foolishness to offset the pressure.

Adults often nag young people to settle down and become serious. Some people distrust happiness as if it were invented by the devil. However, others appreciate the fact that having a good time is healing medicine, which makes life a full trip.

Fools are never serious. They have sunk into the pits of silliness. Smart people learn to see both the work side of the universe and the funny side.

We all have friends that we have cheered up by springing a goofy surprise on them—putting something harmless in their locker, stuffing something cold in their shoe, or just standing in the parking lot and laughing together.

Good friends spread happiness like soft butter. They look for ways to give an extra dose of laughter.

*"When times are good, be happy"* (Eccles. 7:14).

## Some things to think about:

1. Tell how you have cheered someone up.
2. What do you and your friends do for fun?
3. Think of someone you'd like to surprise this week. How could you do it?

# *Being Yourself*

Agnes looked old enough to collect Social Security. If you stopped by to see her, you could count on open hospitality. She was always pushing cookies at you, asking about the family, telling you about the Chicago Bears.

If you dared ask Agnes how she liked your hair or shoes, you were in for a treat. Agnes would tell you directly, honestly and politely. No one asked Agnes hoping to get a compliment. But if you really wanted to know, you could count on Agnes to tell you how she felt.

What you saw was what you got. That's why her friends liked her. Agnes didn't try to fool you, impress you or lie to you. She knew how to be herself in a kind, loving way.

That seems to be the trademark of good friends. You can depend on their genuineness. They never try to take advantage of a friend by lying to him. They don't attempt to exaggerate what they do: like how far they ran or how much money they have. Good friends don't have to pretend with each other.

Being honest doesn't mean being rude. You don't have to say "Your shoes stink" or "Did you get a free comic book with that shirt?" But a good friend does not lie, cheat, steal from or abuse his friends.

Good friends are comfortable to be around. We don't have to always be on our guard when we are with them. That might be an excellent definition of a friend: someone we are comfortable with.

Craig was just the opposite. He wanted to slide into a certain social group because he thought they were cool. Soon he was buying clothes he couldn't afford, combing his hair a different way and actually going places he didn't want to be. Craig saw his goal and was willing to sacrifice to get there.

Unfortunately, what Craig was sacrificing was himself. He was becoming a phony. Before long the new group disliked him, his old friends were disgusted, and even Craig could barely stand the image in his mirror.

It isn't easy to be yourself, especially when you are changing and aren't sure exactly *who* you are. But it's still important to be honest. No one enjoys dishonest people.

As good friends we are open and honest. People will enjoy having us near because they don't have to guess what we are like. We will not be friendly today and pretend not to know them tomorrow. We will not promise to help and then refuse to show up.

Being yourself permits you to give honest answers and actions.

*"An honest answer is like a kiss on the lips"* (Prov. 24:26).

## Some things to think about:

1. Tell one instance of your deciding to do it your way rather than trying to please others.
2. On a scale of one to ten, where do you rate at being yourself?

# *Not an Athlete*

What if you're not a great athlete? What if you aren't tall enough or large enough or even fast enough to start on the school team? Suppose you aren't as coordinated as you would like to be. Does that change the way you feel about yourself?

Feeling like you don't measure up may be one of the most widespread problems faced by teenagers. From their earliest grade-school memories, young people who look the least athletic have been chosen last for baseball, soccer and basketball teams. It doesn't take long for them to realize that athletically they are a step behind. Almost immediately they translate that to mean they are inferior. *Almost immediately.*

By the time they reach high school, they might have a full-fledged complex. That feeling is made worse if the community, the school system and parents treat athletes like Greek gods. Because of this pressure, many grown-ups feel like inadequate adults. They were among the less athletic in school, and have never been able to resolve that problem.

Schools like to brag about their students who have been helped through the athletic program. There is no doubt about it, many students really excel in this area. However, some schools may be afraid to face the fact that a large number of students are emotionally hurt because of the strong emphasis on athletics.

There are several ways to pull this situation back into proper balance. It begins by adjusting the way we think about ourselves. If we control the way we see ourselves, no one can make us feel less valuable.

Can we accept the fact that character is more important than athletic ability, test scores, or money? Honesty, kindness, thoughtfulness, godliness and friendliness are only a few of the qualities that give a person real value. The Bible places these points at the head of the list.

We can become involved in other activities that might give us satisfaction. Music clubs, chess clubs, student senate, movie clubs and woodshop are only a start. Your choice is not athletics or nothing. "Nothing" is a dull, distorted life. If you refuse to become involved in other activities, you are saying that athletics is the only important thing in life.

Don't become bitter at athletes, coaches or the program. They do have a place. Many of those dedicated to sports are people of outstanding character. Shake their hands, congratulate them and be cheerful. But at the same time, pursue the avenues which will give you a sense of fulfillment. Bitterness will do us more harm than any athletic program can begin to do.

Enjoy exercise—especially in a non-competitive setting. But always keep your eyes on the values that make life worthwhile. No one can take your character away. That's what makes you extremely important.

In God's value system the willingness to be a caring, helpful friend is about a hundred notches higher than the ability to pole vault.

*"Therefore, as God's chosen people, holy and dearly loved, clothe yourselves with compassion, kindness, humility, gentleness and patience"* (Col. 3:12).

## Some things to think about:

1. List some good aspects of the athletic program in your school.
2. How would you improve the athletic program in your school?
3. List some programs which you would like to see started in your school.

# Buy Me a Car

There are three things that will change your personality more than anything else: war, famine and cars. Let's talk about cars. A license saying you can drive four to eight cylinders around will show what you are really like.

For some it's the first evidence that they have serious brain damage. Behind a wheel they lose all common sense—drive past stop signs, over medians and even through plowed cornfields. A close relative of mine backed out of the driveway and smashed into the principal's car.

Most young people drive well, but a few bounce around from lane to lane. The ones who have trouble catching on or treat a vehicle like a surfboard make it tough on the others. That is why car insurance is so high.

The ability to drive a car could create a serious dent in your relationship with your parents. After age sixteen a large amount of time is spent discussing cars. Parents want to know who drove on the lawn, who spilled malt on the car floor and how hamburger wrappers got stuck to the rear window. In turn, teenagers want to know if they can have the car on Saturday night (and Sunday morning), who will pay for the gas, and if they can paint a racing stripe on the new Buick.

Car-world is fast moving and can lead to constant arguments. If you want more fun out of driving, it might be well to consider several guidelines.

1. *Your parents don't owe you a car.* Consequently, any help they might give you should be appreciated. The more you express your appreciation, the better your relationship.

2. *Volunteer your help.* Offer to put gas in the car before your parents ask about it. It throws them off guard. All displays of generosity on your part tend to leave them defenseless and willing to cooperate.

3. *Wash the car.* Few parents can say no to a teenager with a rag in one hand and a wax can in the other. Thoughtfulness turns parents into bean dip.

4. *Be on time.* Parents are impressed with certain modes of simple behavior. When a teenager arrives home on time, his/her parents see traces of adulthood. It causes them to feel warm all over.

5. *Recite the insurance oath.* "Teenagers who get too many tickets end up with insurance policies that won't fit in their glove compartment." The premiums charged to careless teen drivers are *enormous.*

6. *Thank you and please.* Too many teenagers develop speech impediments that prevent them from verbally expressing their gratitude. Young people who get along with their parents are the ones who soon outgrow that defect.

In most cases parents are good people. They enjoy showing respect and do love getting it in return. Smart teenagers are taking the time to live at peace with mothers and fathers who sincerely love them.

*"A wise son brings joy to his father, but a foolish son grief to his mother"* (Prov. 10:1).

## Some things to think about:

1. How often do you need to use a car?
2. What courtesy rules for cars have worked well in your family?
3. How do you express appreciation to your parents?

# Sacrifice by a Friend

Terry is the kind of friend everyone appreciates. He enjoys hamburgers, but if everyone wants pizza, you can count him in. And Terry never complains about the sacrifice. It is no big deal for him to give in.

Not that Terry is a doormat. He has things he likes to do and he isn't afraid to say what he thinks. But he is willing to go along with others just to be a friend.

Kelly goes even further than that. She actually plans ways to make her friends happy. Often Kelly volunteers to take her car because she knows that makes it easier for everyone else. Her friends love to hear from her because they know she tries hard to cooperate and make things enjoyable for the others.

You can't beat a friend who is willing to sacrifice part of himself to make you happy. You want to be with that person whenever you can.

That's part of the reason millions of young people are drawn to Jesus Christ. He isn't a big dictator telling everyone what to do. Jesus was willing to pay—and pay greatly—to show His friendship to us. Dying on a cross for His friends—and His enemies—was to pay the greatest price for the people He loved.

All of us can be part of that special friendship by putting our faith in Jesus Christ. It's a simple process, and when we do it, we know there is closeness between us and the Son of God. That closeness will last through the rest of our lives and forever.

We know we are sinners. That doesn't need a long argument. We have done so many harsh and mean things that we seldom doubt our ability to mess up.

To become a Christian we need to ask Jesus Christ to forgive us our sins, to come into our lives and to give us a place in heaven with Him.

Naturally, we have to mean it. We can't simply rattle off words. But when we do ask Him to come into our life, He enters and begins to make changes. He helps us remove the selfishness, the anger, the bad attitudes and long list of uglies that we frequently harbor inside.

When we genuinely deal with the living God and invite Him to be in charge of our lives, He begins to make a difference immediately. We *want* to follow Him because

He's the kind of friend we enjoy being with. We also discover quickly that we can look to Him for leadership and He won't let us down. We begin to see life through Jesus' eyes and everyday things take on a whole new significance. We hate sin. Our attitudes about people and things get straightened out as our new hunger to know Jesus better draws us to read His word.

All of this begins by believing that Jesus, God's Son, made the ultimate sacrifice for us.

*"Greater love has no one than this, that one lay down his life for his friends"* (John 15:13).

## Some things to think about:

1. Name some qualities about Jesus Christ that make Him a good friend.
2. How does Jesus Christ influence your life?

# Evil Friends

Some friendships stink. All that two people who are evil have in common is their satisfaction in doing things that are mean or cruel or evil. They like to get drunk or pick on people or steal. They are friends in every sense of the word. Unfortunately, it is a friendship which leads to trouble.

Friendships are hard to break after they have become tied tightly. It's better to choose carefully before the friendship begins. If two people are continually sharing trouble, they need to stop, because after a while neither can see clearly. Everything wrong seems right to them, and they lose track of what they are doing wrong. Soon both of them end up in a mess and aren't sure how they got there.

A young girl broke up with two of her friends because she didn't want to travel that recklessly. Her friends were shoplifting "just a little." They were flirting with boys much older than they, and she didn't enjoy the pressure. The three were good friends. Each was usually helpful and thoughtful. But this young girl refused to let those qualities blind her to the evil things her friends were doing. The trouble was too threatening, so she took control of her own life and refused to do anything that was wrong no matter what they thought. That decision made her strong.

Many of us are not that wise or that decisive. We go with the flow.

Two of the world's most famous friends were King Herod and Pilate. They had always been enemies until one day they discovered an evil that both of them enjoyed. Each of them put Jesus Christ on trial. They ridiculed the Son of God, called Him names, made fun of His appearance and agreed He was scum.

A great pair, these two. After that experience, they became fast friends. Herod and Pilate loved rejecting Jesus Christ together.

*"Then Herod and his soldiers ridiculed and mocked him. Dressing him in an elegant robe, they sent him back to Pilate. That day Herod and Pilate became friends—before this they had been enemies"* (Luke 23:11, 12).

## Some things to think about:

1. Do you know someone who is in the wrong crowd, who would be a much finer person around other people?
2. How do you muster courage to leave friends who are a bad influence?
3. What should you look for when making friends?

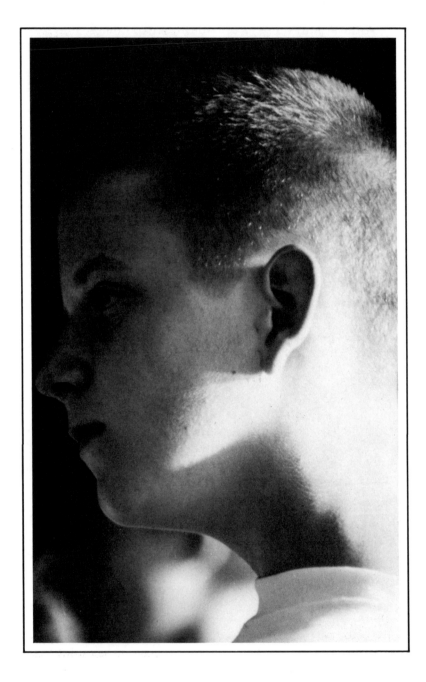

# The Spirit-Connection

Tough decisions. Alcohol, drugs, cars, sex, schools, marriage, careers, faith, finances—the list is long enough to become depressing. The pressure is so great that thousands crack from so many hard choices.

Some young people no longer want to discuss the issues that bother them the most. Talking about it only gives them a headache and they don't seem to arrive at any conclusions.

It's a fact. There aren't any easy answers. But that doesn't mean there isn't any help. There is a spiritual connection which gives new purpose and direction to life. By listening to that influence, this journey begins to make sense and priorities start to fall into place.

When you became a Christian, you asked Jesus Christ to come into your life. At that point you received the Holy Spirit, which Jesus promised. The Spirit of truth came inside of you and took up residence. After that happened, the world was no longer an empty place.

There is more to life than what you can get or grab for yourself. That's a relief, because living becomes boring when it's simply every person for himself.

The Spirit of God quietly counsels us, especially in tough decisions. There is no voice screaming, "Don't touch that!" or "You better vote Independent." Rather, for those who are Christians, there is influence on one's conscience. The moving of the Spirit on our minds and feelings helps direct us to make good decisions.

Don't expect the Spirit to bark at you. Don't expect the Spirit to force you to do anything. But the Spirit will furnish guidance if you want it.

Life is spiritual as well as physical. Jesus said that man does not live on bread alone (Luke 4:4). Those who live only for the things around them—the kicks they can get, the thrills of the moment, the cash they can carry—end up living hollow, disappointing lives.

Living in the Spirit doesn't cancel out our fun, but He will keep us balanced so we won't miss out on having a full life.

Today I read about a famous surfer and genius who went to prison for theft and murder. After 18 years in the penitentiary he now faces life on parole. The Spirit of God could have saved him from a painful existence if he had known God and obeyed Him.

Choices are hard to make. By accepting the Spirit-connection, we begin to fit choices into a wholesome pattern.

*"And I will ask the Father, and he will give you another Counselor to be with you forever—the Spirit of truth. The world cannot accept him, because it neither sees him nor knows him. But you know him, for he lives with you and will be in you"* (John 14:16, 17).

## Some things to think about:

1. How has God helped you with decisions?
2. How do you find out God's direction?

# Slow to Pop
# Your Top

Five teenagers jumped into a beat-up '75 Chevy and were driving around town. They had nothing to do but kill time. They made one stop to pick up several cans of pop and decided to cruise some more.

They were old friends so they joked, horsed around, even yelled a few things out the window that their parents wouldn't have been proud of. High school pals . . . laughing every chance they got at everything they saw.

In the backseat Jeff and Steve were crunched against Mark. They began pushing each other in a good-natured way as they usually did. Suddenly without thinking Jeff turned his pop can upside down and poured root beer all over Steve's lap.

Mark broke into hysterics as Steve struggled to dump some pop back on Jeff. Everyone laughed and even Steve managed to force a wide grin.

Steve's smile was different because it covered a hurt that was growing inside. He resented Jeff's prank and wanted to get even, but he couldn't.

By the time they dropped Steve off at his house, everyone had calmed down. Steve sloshed up his porch steps as the Chevy drove off. At the top of the steps Steve stopped and started to smile. It was pretty funny, he thought. He didn't like it, but it was funny. Besides, Steve remembered, he had done his share of stupid things to his friends.

There was no sense getting burned over this one. His friends meant a lot to him—too much for him to get out of joint because of a dumb prank.

*"Hatred stirs up dissension, but love covers over all wrongs"* (Prov. 10:12).

## Some things to think about:

1. What kind of practical jokes do your friends play?
2. If things get dangerous or out of hand, what should you do?
3. Do you find it easy to forgive?

# Need Some Answers

There are a million decisions to make, and sometimes there is no one to talk to. The Bible is excellent at speaking to many of our needs. Below are a few of the pressing questions young people ask. With each question is a Bible verse. Be sure to look up these passages and decide for yourself what they say.

We seldom have easy answers, but these verses can help us think.

My friends drink on the weekends, even my Christian friends. It's hard to know what to do.                                          Eph. 5:18

Andy is a special person, I love to be with him. He wants to have sex but isn't too pushy. What should I do?                         1 Cor. 6:18

There is a policeman in our town who is out to get teenagers. My friends are very rude to him and it seems to make him meaner. Frankly, I am rude, too.                                                  Rom. 13:1, 2

Some days I feel like a loser. There isn't anything I can do well. I even get so I hate to try because people will only laugh at me. Is it possible that some people are useless?                          1 Cor. 12:4–11

My friends laugh at the Korean twins who attend school. I try to stay out of it, but it's tempting to make fun of them.                                           1 Pet. 2:17

| | |
|---|---|
| I'm getting serious about a guy and I know he isn't a Christian. I don't know if he's the kind of person I should marry. | 2 Cor. 6:14 |
| How do I know if I am a Christian? I sit in church but I'm not sure anything has "happened" to me. | Rom. 10:10–13 |
| Some things I have done in the past still bug me. How do I get God to forgive me? | 1 John 1:9 |

| My friends are trying drugs, but I'm afraid of what it might do to my mind. | Rom. 12:1 |
|---|---|
| It's hard to imagine that God loves me. He may tolerate me, but I can't believe He really loves me. | Rom. 5:8 |

# *Burning Out*

Do you know of two people who were great friends for a little while? They did everything together, had a lot in common and were practically inseparable. Day or night, busy or just hanging out, you were sure to find them with each other.

Then suddenly, after running around together like Siamese twins, their relationship fell apart. Here today and gone tomorrow. Why did it collapse when their friendship had seemed so strong? Maybe it was because they were too thick and simply burned out.

If friends are not careful, they can spend too much time together and wreck their relationship. They lose their room to breathe, as they suffocate an otherwise terrific friendship.

They forget a basic plank in the rules of relationship. It applies to partners, married couples, businessmen, boyfriends and girlfriends, to name a few. When a friendship is smothered by being together too often, burnout is almost always the result.

When that happens, the two friends usually back off, confused and disappointed. They don't know what has gone wrong, but they do know things are not the same. Bewildered, they go in different directions, having lost a close friendship that could have been maintained.

Some people can't stop the burnout from coming. They sense that the relationship is tied too tightly and they are hurting each other by being too close. Despite that, they refuse to back off and simmer down.

It has become a type of addiction. They think they can't get along without the other person. Consequently, they begin to strangle the relationship they want.

Smart people see it coming. To protect their relationship they make a few less phone calls. They still go over to their friend's house, but not quite as often. They don't invite their friend along every time they step out the door. When they need a partner in class or at a game, they start asking someone else.

Breathing room won't hurt a healthy relationship. Instead, it will make the time you spend together twice as valuable. It also allows each person to learn from the others and to bring that new experience into the friendship they already enjoy.

Many couples who go steady express the same frustration. They complain that this friend is always around. They can't do anything without the friend hanging on them. When they say that, you know the relationship is in trouble. They are choking to death for lack of air.

If you have a special relationship, give an extraordinary gift—give your friend room to breathe.

*"Seldom set foot in your neighbor's house—too much of you, and he will hate you"* (Prov. 25:17).

## Some things to think about:

1. List some guidelines for close friends. How often should you be together, etc.?
2. Have you known close friends who backed off and their friendship was helped? Explain.

# *Friends and Faith*

"I like my circle of friends," Darcey explained. "But I don't feel free to share my faith in Jesus Christ with them. I'm afraid I'll come across as a religious nut. Do I have to talk about my faith?"

Millions of teenagers are asking this same question. How can you keep your friends if you thank God for cupcakes, sing hymns on your way to the movies and carry your offering envelope in your top pocket? The answer is easy. You can't keep friends that way and you probably shouldn't.

However, most friendships will allow us to express our faith in Jesus Christ. That is if we will put a few guidelines into place.

First, ask yourself if you *are* a religious nut. Don't brush that question aside as being ridiculous. There is no excuse for rudeness no matter what the situation. Friendship means we are thoughtful and polite. If we are crass or obnoxious, we are not showing Jesus to our friends. Don't even mention your faith until you have mastered a fair degree of civil behavior.

The second thing to remember is that a friendship shows mutual respect for feelings, beliefs and opinions. After we get to know someone, he will listen to subjects that are important to us. If he refuses to tolerate how we feel, we don't consider that friendship much to brag about. Friendship is based on caring. Caring means we want to know what the other person thinks. A huge part of what we think is based on what we believe. Of course, good friends want to know what we believe. If they don't, that friendship needs a transfusion.

No one who respects us will object when we say we believe in heaven. Friends would like to hear about our conversion experience or our goals to serve Christ. Casual or distant friends might have trouble accepting it, but close friends want to understand what makes us tick. We would also like to know what they believe.

If we act or feel superior to our friends, we'll discover they probably don't care much about our faith. But that would be rude on our part, anyway. We don't announce that we are here to be examples for others to follow. Such a declaration would turn most teenagers off.

Get to know people and share your interests. That's at the core of a good friendship. If you are sharing, it is only a matter of time until you bring up your faith in Jesus Christ.

*"We loved you so much that we were delighted to share with you not only the gospel of God but our lives as well, because you had become so dear to us"* (1 Thess. 2:8).

## Some things to think about:

1. What Christian do you admire? Why?
2. Do you have a Christian friend that you feel especially close to?
3. Are you careful to avoid rudeness when explaining your faith?

# A Divorced Family

You can see the pain on the faces of young people who have had their families torn in half. They try to smile, shrug it off and go on. But often their eyes give it away. It's hard to cover up the hurt in one's eyes.

A few of us are glad our parents divorced. But even in those cases, the agony is real. Two parents together, loving, caring, sharing—that seems like the natural way. Parents standing side by side at graduation, at our wedding sounds better.

Divorce leaves its mark on most of the teens it affects. Divorce has a way of messing up your plans, your future, your dreams. Often young people become bitter. Why couldn't their parents make it? Why couldn't they patch it up, find help, tie it back together like adults are supposed to?

But they didn't. And their teenagers are left to make the best of a bad deal. Large numbers of young people find it hard to learn to trust again after their parents divorce. Their vocabulary changes, and they begin saying "maybe," "if" and "we'll see." Afraid to depend on anything, they struggle to feel secure again.

For some it might be easy to choose sides in a divorce. But normally that's not fair. In most cases both parents have contributed considerably to the problem. When the break finally comes, it is hard to identify what really started the problem in the first place.

The natural response is to blame the father. Usually he is the one who packs his bags and leaves the house. But he may or may not have been the major reason for the split. Assigning blame and hurling accusations won't accomplish much, especially after the divorce is final.

Through this tough struggle, many teenagers learn to love both parents again. Holding grudges and nursing wounds only leads to bitterness. Life is filled with too much happiness to have it weighed down by carrying a chip on our shoulder.

Jesus Christ says it's all right to forgive both of our parents even if one of them caused most of the trouble. We have the freedom to forgive our parents. That's one of the special gifts of being a Christian. Besides being free to forgive them, we are actually *told* to forgive them in God's Word. If we don't, we will mainly be hurting ourselves.

Divorce has enough of its own distress. We can't let it hurt us every day, because we can learn to love again.

Sometimes we have to be separated from one of our parents because of abuse. Possibly they abuse drugs, alcohol or people—maybe even us. If separation is the only way, then we'll have to accept it and have good attitudes. We can set ourselves free from hate by forgiving our parents—even from a distance.

There are millions of happily married couples who come from divorced parents. They shake off the bad experiences they have seen and build on the good ones. The foundation, or base, of their new life is the ability to forgive. Forgiveness lets us start all over again.

*"Be kind and compassionate to one another, forgiving each other, just as in Christ God forgave you"* (Eph. 4:32).

## Some things to think about:

1. How can a teen resolve hard feelings toward his divorced parents?
2. What can a teen do to help his parents through and after divorce?
3. How can a teen help his friend whose parents are divorced?

# Coaches Are People, Too

There is little middle ground when we talk about coaches. We tend to either put them on pedestals or knock them to the ground. It's hard to be indifferent about them or their personalities.

We all know coaches who are interested primarily in the students' welfare. If something isn't good for the kids, the coaches don't want it. They are people-centered.

Others are tied to a program, and the students are simply a way to make the athletic department look like a winner. That sounds harsh, but it's true. Pressure comes from every side. Parents, board members, businessmen all want victories. If the coach is going to keep his job, he has to try to make everyone happy. That's where the distortion comes in.

Tony's case is too typical. He played basketball during his freshman year. His natural touch and ball handling were impressive. However, in his sophomore year he decided to take extra classes in math, so he dropped out of basketball.

The coach talked to him about going out, but Tony had made up his mind. Frustrated, the coach began to pressure Tony. Still the boy felt secure in his decision. Tony didn't play his last two years and the coach never spoke to him again.

That wasn't true in Rick's case. His father went to the coach before Rick entered high school and asked, "What do you think? Can Rick play on the varsity here?"

Leaning forward at his desk, the coach told the father, "I've seen Rick and I know he can play here. But don't push him. He doesn't belong on the court unless he will enjoy the game."

The second coach wanted to win, too, but he was able to slide sports into its proper place in life. The athletic program is a valuable addition, but only an addition. Sports are far down the line in a list of real values.

Many schools have coaches like the second one. They try to respect the needs of individuals. If you have a coach who is caring, give him a happy "hello." He or she is a real person who tries to keep life balanced.

Maybe Jesus was saying that one person is more important than an entire sports program. The one person who does not play sports is just as important as the ninety-nine who do.

*Jesus said, "Suppose one of you has a hundred sheep and loses one of them. Does he not leave the ninety-nine in the open country and go after the lost sheep until he finds it?"* (Luke 15:4).

## Some things to think about:

1. Do you know a caring coach? Tell about him.
2. If you were a coach, what would be your priorities?
3. What sport have you enjoyed participating in? Why was it fun?

# Talk About Your Friends

Tonight might be the perfect time to talk about your friends. They mean so much, they should not be ignored. Friends are on your mind and if you admit it, also in your heart. It wouldn't be natural if you didn't talk about them.

The perfect time to talk about your friends is when you are talking to God. Don't wait for the *big emergency*. Any normal day and any subject will do. Talk about their health, their family, their spirits—even their finances. Tell God about your friends' dreams and their need to pick out a school. God isn't just interested in tornadoes and wars. He likes to hear about relationships, caring and geometry classes.

Talking to God about our friends opens a treasure chest of possibilities. For one thing it helps our friends. God does act and answer prayers. Each of us would like to send a generous dose of help in the direction of our friends.

It also helps us keep a good attitude toward our friends. Talking to God protects us from becoming upset, short-tempered and unreasonable. Prayer has a way of mellowing us and taking the sharp edge off our relationships.

Because we talk to God about our friends, we can tell them we do. There is nothing wrong with giving them good news. They will feel better knowing someone is pulling for them.

Personal relationships are some of the most rewarding parts of life. Praying for your friends is getting extremely personal about people you appreciate.

*"Dear friend, I pray that you may enjoy good health and that all may go well with you, even as your soul is getting along well"* (3 John 2).

## Some things to think about:

1. Do you think God has helped your friends at certain times? Tell about it.
2. Do you have friends or family who pray for you?

# Learning to Trust

When Sandy was sixteen, her parents decided to split. Looking back later, she could see some signs that a divorce was coming, but at the time Sandy was devastated. Everything was going well; then one day her parents became angry and decided to separate. Her father moved out; her mother became depressed and cried most of the time.

For Sandy, the changes were almost immediate. There was only one parent to talk to, and she was barely stable. The money drain was instantaneous—like pulling the stopper in the sink. Her family never had been rich, but now there was nothing to "grease the wheels." Soon her mother was talking about moving to another house, possibly another neighborhood; and that meant changing schools.

It made Sandy realize how much she was dependent on things. She had dreamed of a car to drive to school—any tank would do. But even that fantasy was gone.

When she tried to sort things out, Sandy knew it was the lost, hurt people that meant the most. Her dad was never around and her mother was practically a basket case. Sandy wasn't much better herself. She stayed in her room many evenings and cried herself to sleep too often.

After that it was difficult for Sandy to trust people. She had watched someone she loved disappear like a poor magic act. It would be crazy to trust anyone if he could hurt her that much.

Instead of her usual outgoing manner with people, she became like a timid kitten, retreating whenever friends came around.

That was until Tonya took over. Tonya felt she had waited long enough for Sandy to come out of her crack in the wall. She began kidding with Sandy again, stopping by to take her to the game. She put melting ice cream in Sandy's locker just to get a response—*any* response.

It wasn't all fun and games, though. Sometimes Sandy ran the other way or hid in the boiler room, but Tonya refused to quit. Inch by inch and then foot by foot Sandy started to give in. The injured and bruised soul started to trust people again—even if she still had a lump in her throat.

Friends are better than an army. When Humpty Dumpty falls off the wall, his friends can help put him back together again—if Humpty will let them.

*"If one falls down, his friend can help him up"* (Eccles. 4:10).

## Some things to think about:

1. How do you learn to trust when it's hard?
2. Have you befriended someone after his parents' breakup? Tell about it.
3. Has someone befriended you when you were hurting? Tell about it.

# *Popularity*

Which would you rather have: two hundred friends or five? If you answered five, you probably have a more realistic outlook on life. It's possible to have two hundred acquaintances, even companions, and have no friends. No one close. No one to share with. No one to call late at night.

It isn't hard to understand why the class president gets depressed. Everyone likes him but maybe no one is close to him. He might be happy in a crowd, but take the crowd away and he becomes terribly lonely.

That could also explain why some popular teenagers practically fall apart once they leave high school. They were comfortable with a large group and they "performed" well. But once their security structure was lost, they were barely able to function.

This doesn't mean that popular teenagers are bound to become chimney soot later. However, they do seem to survive better if they can establish a core of five or more close friends. Impersonal crowds are not enough to sustain most people.

Because we misunderstand this happy little principle, millions of all ages are working hard in the wrong direction. They consider success the ability to get on top. Instead, personal success really comes from collecting and maintaining a handful of friends who actually care.

It's difficult to have more than a few genuine friends. It takes a great deal of time and energy to support a close friendship. We have to give, repair, invest, smooth over, sacrifice, tolerate and plan for our friends. There are only so many people we can afford to do all that for. We can sustain a larger number of acquaintances, but close friends need to be nurtured.

By aiming for everyone we fail to hit anyone. Popularity looks great, but many will tell you it isn't the way it appears. A person can perform in front of twenty thousand people only to return to an empty apartment and be miserably lonely.

Go for the handful. Make five or six friends special in your life and don't worry about the hundreds or thousands.

## Some things to think about:

1. In your school, who is the most popular?
2. What do you like about your best friends?

# An Unusual Friend

Friends come in a wide variety of packages. They dress in red shorts and wear orange tops. They think nothing of eating pizza by the boxful and drinking soda by the quart. Friends laugh late into the night, park their cars in your father's driveway, and throw snowballs at passing vehicles.

Those are the people friends. The kind that walk, talk and play drums late at night.

There is another type of friend. One that never changes its mind, spills popcorn on the floor or leaves the door open. This friend is a book and we call it the Bible.

The Bible is packed with help, counsel and even advice. It tells us about personal relationships, love, passion, sex and marriage. There are plenty of guidelines, examples, lessons and captivating stories. Its characters are real. They hope, hate, win, lose, have children and fall out of windows.

And just the time you feel yourself becoming unglued, it pops up with a passage that helps hold you together.

The Bible is frank. It calls evil, evil and good, excellent. It doesn't kid around about what is wrong. Friends are like that. It's also filled with encouragement and praise. The Bible tells us when we have "done well."

If you want to know more about relationships, this book will tell you about the big ones. It introduces us to what God is really like and how much He cares. We hear about the Son of God and get to meet Him. It tells us how to invite Jesus Christ into our lives. How to have our sins forgiven. How to begin on the road to making Jesus the Lord of our lives.

The Bible doesn't say much about car repair, but it might stop us from kicking the hubcaps or trying to catch the driver who speeds past us. It doesn't mention mutual funds, but it talks about the problem of loving money.

A book can be a friend—especially this book. It's polite and won't jump out and grab your arm. It won't make you read it. But those who take the time find strength for today and forever.

Maybe you will want to start in the book of Proverbs. The Gospel of Luke is especially clear about the life of Christ. (You can save the Levitical sacrifices and the tribes of Israel for later.)

One step at a time, one day at a time, start getting acquainted with a book that can become an unusual friend.

*"Your word is a lamp to my feet and a light for my path"* (Ps. 119:105).

## Some things to think about:

1. How has the Bible helped you?
2. Give some hints for using the Bible.
3. What parts of the Bible are your favorites?

# Great Grandparents!

It's surprising how many teenagers turn to their grandparents when they go to high school. If they have kept close contact over the years, it's easy. If not, many still make an effort to get to know them.

Melissa visits the grave of her grandfather when she feels mellow and just wants to be alone. It isn't morbid. She merely wants to connect with someone who was special.

Grandparents are gold mines. They may not have wealth, but they are usually rich in acceptance, patience, pride and understanding. They have a way of making a teenager feel special. If a young person is having friction at home or trouble communicating, his grandparents' home often serves as a safety zone.

As teenagers stretch out to become more independent, many of them like to move toward their grandparents. Grandparents have a way of listening without judging. They usually get excited about accomplishments without being uptight about your bedroom or your homework. Another neat thing about grandparents is that they are pleased to see you drop over. They need you too.

Grandparents also serve to give teens an added sense of identity. Teens can hear how Granddad worked on the railroad or how Grandmother cleaned chickens when she was a little girl. Young people can sense the fact that their foundations go back many years and they love to hear about it. They know the grandparents are not just gnats on the windshield of life—here today and gone in a second.

Not every grandparent can offer this feeling of belonging, though. Some don't communicate well. Others don't seem comfortable with the charging energy of teenagers. Many grandparents live far away and bridge that gap by writing or sending tapes directly to their grandchildren. The young people who take time to answer back build an inner strength by being connected with people who care.

If you examine the writings of teenagers, it is interesting to see how frequently they refer to their grandparents. For millions, this is the time when one or two grandparents die. It's the teen's first experience at seeing part of his family pass out of this life and enter eternity. Young people are normally sobered and hurt by it. But it's a concrete lesson in how temporary life and its relationships are.

Don't be too surprised if you feel a strong need to reach out and improve your contact with grandparents. It may become one of the most rewarding relationships you will ever have.

A young Christian in the Bible, Timothy, watched his grandmother's faith and it helped him follow Jesus Christ. We all know of people who have seen their grandparents walk close to Christ. We also know of teenagers who have shown their faith to their grandparents.

*"I have been reminded of your sincere faith, which first lived in your grandmother Lois and in your mother Eunice and, I am persuaded, now lives in you also"* (2 Tim. 1:5).

## Some things to think about:

1. Name some outstanding qualities of your grandparents.
2. What are some ways teens can build bridges with grandparents?
3. Do you have friends who have adopted an older person to fill the role of grandparent? Tell about it.

# Herman the Hermit

There may be a few people who are tickled purple to spend every day alone. But not most of us. Those who have wild birds flying in the house, those who are mass murderers, and people who eat onion and sardine sandwiches should stay alone. The rest of us need someone to rub elbows with.

Unfortunately, there is an occasional teenager who has chosen to go the Herman the Hermit route. Most who sink into isolation would rather mix with friends, but they have decided to stop taking risks. They don't want to take the chance of being rejected, so they slide through the cracks and disappear.

If they play the Hermit role too often, their people skills start to rust. They then find it harder to mingle and might give it up altogether.

When the problem becomes that acute, drastic steps have to be taken. The best remedy rests with Herman. He must bring himself to go to church and social events whether he likes it or not. Once there, Herman needs to begin talking, helping and searching. Soon he or she (Sherman?) will find a nitch that he enjoys. Even if he doesn't believe it will happen, he must try anyway. By staying in his fort, he only makes it more difficult to circulate later.

Force yourself to stay in touch with people. Most of us need it to sustain our mental health. Don't mess with that risk.

Those of us who have no Hermit complex have a vital job. It's our responsibility to pick out a person who is fading and help him. It may not mean we drag them out of their house by the heels, but that's a possibility.

Certainly, we want to befriend them. Invite Herman to go with you. Offer to drop by for him. This is a first-class ministry for young people. Countless people have been literally rescued from a life of dullness and depression simply because someone showed an interest. Talents, skills, even lives are being wasted because they retreat behind the walls of a lonely room.

We can't make people round out their lives, but we can try to make it easier for them. It's a small price to pay to see others come alive.

*"The Lord God said, 'It is not good for the man to be alone' "* (Gen. 2:18).

## Some things to think about:

1. Have you befriended someone like Herman? Tell about it.
2. Do you know Hermans in other age groups besides teenagers?
3. What are some suggestions for drawing out a Herman?

# *Empty Heads*

Have you met any teenagers who have styrofoam for brains? They are destructive creatures who don't know what to do with themselves. Their weekends are boring. Driving around on back roads and drinking is all they can think of. Once in a while half a dozen will park their cars at a drive-in and they will stand around and grumble.

And the amazing thing is that they pretend everyone else is dull. Millions of young people as well as adults wander through life with little point or purpose. They lack meaning.

However, not all teenagers see their world as a dead-end street. Many have taken the opportunity to get involved in serving others. By contributing in life they have shaken off the blues. By refusing to stand around looking for kicks, they have found a way for life to make sense.

It's amazing how many teenagers you meet who find it exciting to help others. Despite a wall of cynicism, young people are concerned about the injustices and pain they see around them.

Connie is a great example. She has spent the past two summers working with children in the hills of Kentucky. For ten weeks she helped distribute clothing, played games, taught reading and explained the love and forgiveness of Jesus Christ. Connie felt better about her summers than if she had stayed home and cruised.

The same can be said of Mike. He saved his money and traveled to Haiti to help dig wells for two weeks. He felt good about himself, watched sick children drink fresh water, gained a world view, expanded his mind, and drew closer to God.

These were average teenagers. They had no more money, no more brains, no more courage than anyone else. However, they were willing to jump out and find meaning for their lives. They had purpose.

Young people who sit on car hoods sneaking beers all evening are sad sights. They often feel empty in a world that has little to offer them. A life spent looking for kicks is bound to be tasteless.

Mary headed south for the summer to work with inner-city kids in Dallas. Her days were spent teaching children, listening to problems and breaking up fights. She had never seen children who had so little to eat, whose parents abandoned them during the day, who had no place to go.

She learned that she could be important to others. Her life had special meaning because she was not totally self-centered.

It's easy to be empty-headed. To sit around and beat our drum saying, ''Why doesn't someone make me happy?'' But it's a life that is never quite complete.

God has given us the ability to help others. If we waste those talents, it's like throwing part of ourselves away.

*"Each one should use whatever gift he has received to serve others, faithfully administering God's grace in its various forms"* (1 Pet. 4:10).

## Some things to think about:

1. Do you know a teen who is involved in helping others? Tell about it.
2. What do you do to reach out to help someone else?
3. What are some things you could do to reach out to help others?

# A Grouchy Teacher

Have you ever watched a teacher and a student rub each other like sandpaper? They don't get along and never have. There is no single event that sets it off; their personalities simply strike like matches, and fire is often the result.

Somewhere it has probably happened to you—in public school, in private school or even in church. There is something about our nature that guarantees we will eventually collide with certain types of people.

It's part of life and always will be. Even if you try hard to get along with everyone, it still won't work. We need to keep that in mind so we can keep our cool. Friction happens to the best of people. The smart ones learn how to handle it without blowing up.

One of the worst cases I have seen is when a boy decided to get even with his teacher. The teacher may have been totally wrong, but the boy only made it worse. Once he set a course of revenge, he could count on experiencing a great amount of pain.

After making several attempts to embarrass the teacher, the teenager ended up failing the class, barely graduating and feeling bitter toward the school. His anger got out of control and backfired.

It's important to remember that the vast majority of teachers are caring, kind people. Don't let one or two distort your view of the entire lot. Most of us could talk for hours about teachers who have sacrificed to help us.

We then need to accept rudeness and even harshness as part of the human condition. There are many cactus-like personalities out there and we need practice in learning how to deal with them.

Next, promise yourself that you will not let a teacher's behavior hurt your plan. It's his problem; don't let it become yours.

Politely resist any of his absurd demands. Gently and clearly stand up to him if necessary. God gave you some rights, and He created you as a full person, not as a carpet. However, be determined you will not go to war. Students seldom win battles.

Set an example. Your kind approach is not only the right thing to do, it may be a way to bring about a change in the teacher's life. If you become vengeful, you become like the teacher. If you show love, the teacher might become like you.

Pray for yourself (and for the teacher). Because you are open to God's power, pray for yourself first, and invite God to work on your attitude. It's surprising how God will mellow and rearrange the way we think. Then pray for the teacher, asking God to bless him according to His knowledge. That way you will not be judging him, and God will be free to work in his heart.

If the teacher is a walking grouch, he has probably received a ton of abuse in return. Nastiness tends to create nastiness. By handing him love in exchange for his rudeness, we have hope of helping him as well as protecting ourselves.

*"Dear friends, since God so loved us, we also ought to love one another"* (1 John 4:11).

## Some things to think about:

1. Do you know a student who is picked on by a teacher? What should he do?
2. Name five outstanding teachers you have had.

# Guard Your Head

Each of us has had some strange, terrible or even cruel thoughts. We would all be embarrassed if our thoughts were played back to us on video. The pictures we create in our minds may not be good, but many people have the same experience. It's important to know we aren't weird, sick or mad because of what we think.

When we become sexually alive, our hormones send out mental images galloping in crazy directions. It isn't odd to have sexual fantasies. Most of us do. Unfortunately some teenagers don't understand that and begin to think they are bonkers. Worse yet, a few grow into adulthood still believing they have mental problems. Good, healthy people have hurt their own personalities because their thoughts frightened them so badly.

Christian teenagers need to know that if they have sexual fantasies, they are perfectly normal. When your body matures and your sexual desires arise, your mind and imagination are bound to respond. Calm down; you are going through a natural process.

Even among adults, the number who have sexual fantasies is quite high.

For you to want to be held, kissed or even have sex with an attractive, appealing person is no need for undue concern. It happens to all of us. Even often.

Despite the fact that it is normal, we need to take a few precautions. Here are several questions we need to ask ourselves from time to time.

1. *Are we retreating to fantasies in an attempt to escape life?* We can develop a bad habit of avoiding responsibilities by running away from the real world.

2. *Can we turn our backs on what we think?* Self-discipline is a friend to those who use it, and we need to be careful that we don't simply surrender to a life of fantasies.

3. *Are our thoughts beginning to change our actions?* Are we beginning to look at people as purely sex objects? Are we starting to plot and plan ways in which we could carry out our imaginations? It's dangerous and wrong if we cross the line from natural fantasies into a world of action.

Natural or not, we don't have to let our imaginations control us to the point of sin. There's a difference between temptation and sin. Jesus was tempted just like we are—"yet without sin." That's because when a tempting thought flashed into His mind, He said *no* to it and made the choice to think about and do something else. With His power working in our lives, we have the ability to make the same choices Jesus did. No one said this is easy, but it *is possible.*

The realm of sex is tough for teenagers. It's no picnic for adults, for that matter. So why don't we throw off the restraints and do whatever we want? Because the results of sex without boundaries are far worse. God knows that and so should we.

Head games are unpredictable. We need to guard and monitor our own so we don't lose control.

*"It is God's will that you should be holy; that you should avoid sexual immorality; that each of you should learn to control his own body in a way that is holy and honorable, not in passionate lust like the heathen, who do not know God"* (1 Thess. 4:3–5).

## Some things to think about:

1. How do you make your mind think good thoughts?
2. If an unhealthy thought keeps popping into your mind, how can you prevent it?
3. Does what you read affect what you think?

# Bailing Out

No one thought she had a problem in the world. Teresa was always smiling and, except for a few times, seemed generally up and happy. When she took an overdose, the entire student body was shaken.

With Chad it was different. He had withdrawn from the crowd to spend more and more time alone. Despondent, he had little to say, and when he did talk it was downbeat. When he shot himself, many said they had sensed it might happen.

Those stories and ones like it are being repeated all over the country. Thousands of teenagers are killing themselves. Tens of thousands are attempting it and possibly millions have thought about it. Youth speakers tell us that after rallies, assemblies and church services, they find many teenagers waiting to ask questions concerning suicide.

Almost every type of young person thinks about it sooner or later. Active and inactive. Popular and loners. Athletes, academics, actors and the laid-back. Non-Christians and Christians both give it a thought.

National authorities list a number of contributing factors.

1. *A feeling of doom.* They think the future is hopeless. There aren't enough jobs; we are all going to get nuked. They hear it in school, on television and in church. Life looks like a bummer.

2. *Competition.* Young people have fought to play on teams, to get good grades, to earn badges, to get into the gifted program, to be accepted by their peers and their parents. Exhausted, they want to give up.

3. *Lost security.* Too many have lost their stable homes because of divorce. When times get tough, they aren't sure where they can turn.

4. *Battered relationships.* They have seen many people hurt. Their friends, their parents, victims on television. Afraid to trust people, they feel they have no one to lean on.

Throw these four pressures into the pot and add a number of other depressing ingredients and the kettle soon develops a foul stench. We need to reach out and reduce these feelings of hopelessness.

After three suicides in five days and several other attempts, the student body of one high school waged a war against despair. The parents, teachers and students at Bryan High School in Omaha, Nebraska, began a Choose Life program.

In sixteen months eight youths killed themselves in Plano, Texas. Adults and young people there started a network of caring and counseling that all but put an end to the tragedies.

Each of us needs a series of strengths to hold on to in time of unbearable stress.

1. *People who care.* Friends, relatives, small groups mean something special to us. We also need to care about them.

2. *Hopeful goals.* We need a reason to look forward to tomorrow. Maybe even a reason so the next hour makes sense.

3. *Spiritual reality.* Life consists of more than report cards, yearbooks and dates. We need a Force who brings life together. Jesus Christ does that by giving us purpose for today and forever.

Teenagers have a unique way of giving hope to other teenagers. That's part of why we need each other.

God has started to do a good job in us. If we give Him enough time, He will do an even better one.

*"Being confident of this, that he who began a good work in you will carry it on to completion until the day of Christ Jesus"* (Phil. 1:6).

## Some things to think about:

1. Have you known someone who committed suicide?
2. What pressures contribute to a feeling of hopelessness?
3. What would you do if someone came to you and said he was planning suicide?

# Keeping a Boyfriend

Relationships are fragile. They run hot and cold, thick and thin. Without nourishment and care, they can easily go sour and start to stink. That's true whether the friendship is based on shared interests or romance.

Each of us needs to step back and evaluate our friendships from time to time. We should ask ourselves a few frank questions like: Does this relationship cause me more pain than fulfillment? What do I gain from this friendship? How much does it cost me to maintain the closeness we share?

This is true of all friendships. If they constantly drag you down, it's time to break away. Some people keep crummy relationships going and before long their personalities change. The smart ones see what's happening and take control of their lives.

With boyfriends and girlfriends, the questions are extra important. It's easy to get lost in the fog when we have a special affection for someone. A few starter questions might help us get going. Everyone can think of some more that better fit his situation.

Are you happy more than you are sad? Unless you stop and calculate this one, it's easy to miss. We can expect some heavy moments; that's part of having a relationship. However, if you spend more time pouting, frowning and wondering, something needs to change. Either the friendship needs to improve or it needs to go.

Are you the one who gives in all the time? Check this out carefully. We all feel this way sometimes. The crucial phrase is "all the time." If you believe this has become a one-way relationship, you should take stock of the situation. Maybe your friend isn't aware of the lopsidedness. Possibly it isn't even real. A good conversation could clear this up and keep a solid relationship going. What if your friend is basically selfish and you can't talk about it? Then you have a serious problem.

Is this relationship a financial disaster? If the friendship

is dependent on money that you don't have, your future is filled with the uglies. Couples are often drained until the financial loss kills their true feelings for each other.

Talking is the key to solving this problem. The two of you have to be free to discuss real conflicts, and few are more vital than this one. If neither of you can or should afford this relationship, adjustments have to be made.

Does the relationship depend on your moral compromise? If your friend expects you to do things that you feel are wrong, you are swimming in dangerous waters. No one who cares for you has any right to ask you to violate your moral framework. To put it in plainer words: Your body can't be the price you pay to keep this relationship going. Both of you will be sorry this kind of sacrifice was made.

Again, these are things that the two of you can talk about, but you *cannot* compromise. The person who goes against his moral values loses twice: his body loses and his conscience loses. Those are flimsy blocks on which to build a relationship.

Friendships are not strengthened by ignoring the important questions. They are reinforced by honest, open discussion. Neither are they healthy if our friend is talking us into things that we know we should resist. When we really like someone, he sounds very convincing. That's all the more reason to weigh our friend's words carefully.

*"With persuasive words she led him astray; she seduced him with her smooth talk"* (Prov. 7:21).

## Some things to think about:

1. Do you have a relationship that is more painful than happy? Think about what you should do.
2. Do you know a relationship where one person gives in all the time?

# *Partying*

There was a long hallway in Eastern High School. It connected the main building to the gymnasium. The hall was decorated with pictures of famous athletes who had attended that school—many who had starred in sports in Washington, D.C., over the past forty years.

Generally, students hustled down that hall barely noticing one another. Once in a while I happened to see an old man (probably aged fifty) standing alone as the herd stampeded to class.

His clothes were old but neat. He held a short, cold cigar in his hand. Quietly, the expressionless man looked at the pictures on the wall.

After seeing him several times, I asked one of the teachers about the "Charlie Chaplin" character with the half-closed eyes. This was the story I heard.

At one time he had been a student and an excellent athlete there. To this day he still holds a couple of track records. His high school experience was good; he graduated and looked forward to an exciting career in college.

On graduation night a group of friends piled into a car and went out drinking with him. They had a lot to celebrate.

The evening ended with a horrendous noise. They wrapped the car around a tree. No one was hurt too seriously—except the guy who stands in the hall.

About once a week he comes to the high school and stares at his picture and tries to remember what it was like—*before* he went partying.

*"Do not get drunk on wine"* (Eph. 5:18).

## Some things to think about:

1. What percentage of students in your school drink once a week?
2. How do they get alcohol?
3. Does your community have any program for problem drinkers? Explain.

# Ask Him Out

Dating patterns are changing—many for the better. One of the most drastic changes is that more girls are asking guys out. That's a big improvement, freeing up everyone to enjoy life a great deal more.

A few years ago I made the suggestion in a book, *The Great Date Wait*. Not everyone appreciated the idea, but many did and said so. When I speak to youth groups, I bring up the concept and ask them if traditions are changing. They tell me they are. This is part of what I have learned from the groups:

* *It isn't a new idea.* I meet happily married parents and grandparents who started dating when she asked him out. It's been going on for years.

* *It's extremely popular in many countries and in certain corners of the United States.* "Big new idea you have," a teenager with an accent told me. "Girls always ask boys out in my country."

* *Girls who ask guys out enjoy the feeling of independence and confidence.* They appreciate more say in whom they do or don't date. Teenage girls do not see themselves as mindless victims waiting to see whom they have to go with.

* *When girls take the initiative, there are greater possibilities that each person can pay his own way.* This makes it easier to have more dates since the poor guy isn't forced to kick out all the money. It also eliminates the question of whether or not she has to "pay" for the date by compromising physically.

Bobbi was asked out by a boy and they had a great evening together. He picked her up, paid for everything and delivered her back home. The next week she called him, picked him up and paid for everything. They enjoyed both evenings.

* *Expect resistance.* There are a few parents and teenagers who think this is brazen and out of order. Respect their opinions but try to come to your own conclusions.

* *Despite our background and prejudices, there seem to be no serious reasons why girls can't ask guys out.* There is no biblical or social reason why this will not work if we give it a try.

Girls can never be free to select friends for a date until they have the option to ask whomever they wish. They deserve the right to pick friends just as the boys do.

It's something we should think about and discuss.

## Some things to think about:

1. Do you know girls who have asked boys out? What do you think about it?
2. Would your friends go for the idea of girls asking boys out?
3. If you are a boy, would you want to be asked out by a girl?

# *Be Your Body's Best Friend*

Guess how many of your friends are unhappy with their bodies. They think they are too tall, too short, too fat or too thin. The secret word is "too." A vast majority of American teenagers seem to believe their bodies are "too" something.

This is a serious problem that affects mostly the middle or upper class. Few people in third-world or underdeveloped countries suffer from body fixation. They are happy just to have a body.

The pressure to continually alter our bodies has gone bonkers in our society. Much of it is caused by television, beauty contests and magazines. Each showcases what we have come to accept as the "ideal" figure. Continually exposed to those images, we feel obligated to match them. If we don't, we believe we have a failed "body."

It's no small problem that millions are in *daily agony* because they feel they can't measure up. One survey found that 80% of the population had been on a diet by the time they were ten years old. By now you have probably been on several diets.

Teenagers are starving themselves, are in misery, have headaches, are grouchy simply because they cannot match the "image" they see before them. That's a tough road to ride.

Sandra lives in Colorado. She barely manages to cover her frame with a minimal amount of flesh. Any of her friends would tell her that her weight is average to skinny. There aren't two ounces of fat on her body. Despite her friends, she will not be convinced.

Nearly every day Sandra runs, rides bikes, eats rice cakes—all in an attempt to control her weight. She tortures herself trying to reach a goal that, if she reaches it, will be unhealthy for her.

If Sandra becomes too obsessed with control, she may cross the border and become anorexic. That's a serious problem from which people too often die.

Be your body's best friend. If you don't, no one else will. Give yourself some basic guidelines.

*First, decide what would be the healthiest thing for you to do.* Get an image of yourself in the background and aim for good function. No matter how thin you become, you will make everyone unhappy if you are a dragon to be around.

*Second, praise God for your features.* Your nose, ears, chest, and the rest of your body are just great the way they are. In the long run, they will not matter to you, your children or anyone else who is important. Character is worth sweating over, but having long fingers will never stop you from being unhappy.

In very rare cases someone has a serious physical defect and may want to consult his doctor. These are extremely rare.

*Third, give your life a spiritual context.* To live for Jesus Christ helps us take our eyes off ourselves. When we do, we begin to help others. In teaching underprivileged children to read, we tend to forget that we have a "wart" behind our ear lobe.

Bodies are important. But they are only part of the total picture.

*"For physical training is of some value, but godliness has value for all things"* (1 Tim. 4:8).

## Some things to think about:

1. What is "inner beauty"?
2. Do you know people who are hung up on looks? Explain.

# Proud of Your Parents

What in the world are you going to do with your parents? They dress funny, tell sad jokes and like to watch black and white movies. Their idea of fun is to sit around and talk. Their "heroes" are William F. Buckley and Ted Koppel. Their concept of good television is the educational channel. They actually watch films about seals and get excited about press conferences!

Parents live in a world teenagers don't appreciate or understand. Sometimes teens even feel embarrassed by their parents' strange behavior and life patterns. But despite those wide differences, there is usually a warm love buried in the heart of a young person for his or her parents.

Don't be surprise if that special feeling begins to surface more and more over the next few years.

A few teenagers have serious problems with their parents—especially if they have been abused, neglected, or mishandled. It may take an extra dose of the grace of God and possibly some counseling in order for those victims to receive healing for their emotions.

The average teenager carries a trace of pride about his parents. These teens may work hard at keeping the pride smothered, but it's there. In the next four years you will discover yourself picking out graduation pictures, attending a couple of Daddy-Daughter Date nights, maybe crying on your mother's shoulder a few times, looking for your parents in the audience at graduation, or talking to them until two in the morning. The pride you have for your parents will keep growing and you will be glad for it.

Meanwhile, try to appreciate them. Listen to their stories. Hear how far they walked to school. Let them tell you one more time how little allowance they got. And every chance you get, go out with them for a snack, shop with them for clothing, or challenge them to a game of chess—just to see them smile.

Parents are good gifts given directly by God. Each year you can sense that love growing. They have been outstanding parents and terrific people.

*"Parents are the pride of their children"* (Prov. 17:6).

## Some things to think about:

1. What are the best times you have with your parents?
2. Name five things you like about your parents.
3. How can you draw closer to your parents?

# Flying Books

John was the kind of person who enjoyed having fun. He was good-natured, thoughtful and all of the things you like about someone. Probably the only thing he didn't enjoy was being bored.

Our music class in Junior High School was on the third floor in Washington, D.C. The room had large windows that were opened in the spring since we had no air conditioning.

One day when the teacher had been out of class for some time, John got into one of his bored moods. Since he was standing by an open window, he simply grabbed the first stack of books he saw and dropped them out. He laughed gustily as he watched my books sail three floors and smash on the pavement below.

John enjoyed it all the more because they were *my* books.

Naturally, I laughed with John since I didn't want to look like a hardhead. While both of us laughed, I merely handed John a second set of books and encouraged him to toss those out into space.

Automatically John dumped the set of books and they plummeted downward. No sooner had they left his hands than John's face collapsed. His jaw dropped. He gasped as his own set of books hurtled toward the ground below.

In a second John pulled himself together and was his happy self again. He forgave me for handing him his own books and I forgave him for tossing mine. Neither of us said it. We simply felt it.

Forgiving each other is part of what friends do. It helps keep them close.

*"Bear with each other and forgive whatever grievances you may have against one another. Forgive as the Lord forgave you"* (Col. 3:13).

## Some things to think about:

1. Do you have a friend whom you must forgive frequently?
2. Have you forgiven a friend recently? Tell about it.
3. Do you find it easy to apologize?

# Knots on Their Heads

We all have friends who are head-knockers. The only way they learn is by beating their heads against brick walls. Most of them survive—but only after severe skull damage.

If a parent tells this person to be careful and not touch the wet paint, he will immediately rub his finger on it. When a teacher says a paper is due on Thursday, the student wonders what will happen if it gets there on Friday. A no-parking sign is an open invitation.

You could almost admire a head-knocker if it were simply a case of curiosity. Who would discourage a little investigative creativity? The problem is that most of these concrete-bangers carry a feeling of invincibility. They really believe they cannot or will not lose. That attitude leads them to try the craziest escapades.

With that attitude they frequently challenge the police without one thought of getting caught or paying the consequence. They speed, drink, forget to carry their driver's license, refusing to even consider that there might be a penalty to pay.

How often have you heard someone who got into trouble shrug his shoulders and mutter, "I never thought I would get caught."

The police tell me most head-knockers eventually turn around. Generally they mess with the authorities once or twice and don't care to get burned again. The sad ones learn slowly and have to get hurt before they quit pounding their brains.

One head-knocker in a thousand never learns and has to go to jail.

Our adventurous spirit is part of what makes human beings so fascinating. However, that spirit has to be tempered with common sense and a dab of self-preservation. Even a bull can break its neck when charging into stone walls.

"I had to find out everything for myself. I wouldn't listen to anybody." That's what Brad admitted. He was serving nine months in prison as a repeat offender.

Head-knockers have their pride. Unable to accept the experience of others, they must test every rule. Pride will bring them pain. Pride will cause them to hurt others without even thinking.

That is why God is so tough on pride. Few sins are as destructive as this little terror.

God keeps reminding us how harmful pride can be, but the head-knocker has a rebellious spirit and turns away. He has rules to lean on, laws to test out, substances to try, people to push. He finds it hard to listen to God when there is so much to experiment with.

Hopefully he will grow tired of the pain before he gets too many dents in his cranium.

*"Pride goes before destruction, a haughty spirit before a fall"* (Prov. 16:18).

## Some things to think about:

1. Do you know people who won't listen to advice and always find out the hard way? Tell about it.
2. Where do you go for advice?

# How Far Is Too Far?

All teenagers ask the question, How far is too far? And if they don't, they should. It has to be one of the three or four most important subjects on a young person's mind.

No one wants to be left out, and yet no one wants to be a fool either. Where do you draw the line in physical closeness?

There is no answer that will satisfy everyone. There is no safety zone beyond which no one dare travel. Naturally, intercourse before marriage is wrong. There are too many dangers, too little commitment, too many months and years to wait. And, the Bible is clear on calling sex before marriage sin.

But, how much "petting," touching, or even caressing can a couple do and manage to keep control? There is no index to give you the answer. There is no dial-a-solution that can spell it out for you.

Rather than trying to measure the immeasurable, let's look for some guidelines we might apply.

1. *Roaming hands will get you into trouble.* It may sound simple, even innocent, but it's hard to keep it that way. Hands have no conscience. They will merely do whatever a wild brain allows.

2. *Is that all you have to do?* If a date is not planned and all you expect to do is sit around and talk, the relationship is bound to become physical quickly. Is your association based on physical activity? If that has become the thing you have most in common, your friendship has a hollow quality to it.

3. *Where is your physical activity heading and how fast?* Most petting is progressive. It seldom stands still. How quickly is yours advancing? At this rate, how soon will it become more than you had in mind? Is it already further than you are comfortable with?

Sometimes teenagers take an honest look at their physical involvement and realize how unhappy they are. There are few feelings as bad as knowing you have lost control. Once young people have admitted to themselves that they are in further than they intended, some take charge of their lives again. Maybe just in time.

Each of us is weak. Each of us is strong. God is pulling for us, hoping we will choose to use our strengths rather than our weaknesses.

God is cheering for us. *Hold on! Take control! Draw the line!* Don't get hurt in a few moments of foolishness.

*"It is God's will that you should be holy; that you should avoid sexual immorality; that each of you should learn to control his own body"* (1 Thess. 4:3, 4).

## Some things to think about:

1. How do you keep your emotions and activities in control?
2. How can you tell a friend he/she is becoming too physical?
3. Name some guidelines for dating.

# *A Second Look at Going Steady*

It has to be one of the biggest questions young people ask. Going steady has so much appeal that practically every teenager is fascinated by the possibility. After all, the benefits are tremendous.

1. *You have a dependable date.* That comes in handy for special events, lonely weekends and someone to bum around with.

2. *You have someone to care.* When you hurt or are bubbling over with happiness, you have a special person to share it with. Sometimes parents simply are not enough.

3. *You feel wanted.* Can't beat it. It's great to know there is someone in the world who thinks you are cream cheese. Those kinds of people love to have you around.

4. *You have someone to care about.* Unbeatable ingredient. Each of us has a gigantic capacity to love. We often enjoy centering that concern on one outstanding person.

5. *You feel mature.* Wearing a ring or a necklace gives us a sense of adulthood. Teenagers are grown-up and they like to feel that way.

These are only five reasons why going steady is so popular. You may have another one or two to add. It certainly depends on your personality and circumstances.

Let's consider what seem to be the drawbacks. They are well worth thinking over.

1. *It's restrictive.* There are a number of other teenagers who might like to get to know you better if they had the chance. Going steady draws a circle around you and limits some of your friends.

2. *It's obligating.* Many people who go steady act as though they have a heavy stone of responsibility hanging on their neck. They have lost their sense of freedom. They must check with the person with whom they are going steady. There is a constant fear of misunderstanding. We each must choose between freedom and security. They have selected security but have lost something valuable.

3. *It's risky.* Couples going steady may run a higher risk of getting physically involved. Don't laugh too quickly. It's hard to admit but many couples wish they could control themselves better. Casual dates are generally less likely to go too far.

4. *It's heartbreaking.* Sooner or later most couples have to split. Few of them do it without a great amount of pain. Any way it's done is a junker—give the ring back, write a letter, make a phone call. We are talking about tears, aching hearts, sleepless nights, confusion. That's part of the price we pay.

I discussed this in a previous book, *The Great Date Wait*. After looking more closely at the subject, my conclusion is the same: going steady is a bummer.

The young people I have met who are going steady have been the nicest teenagers. I wish you well. Have a terrific time. But it still looks like a loser to me.

Your best bet is to have fun with many friends. Get to know people. But guard your heart until you're in a position to really give it away. Until then your heart is worth protecting.

*"Above all else, guard your heart"* (Prov. 4:23).

## Some things to think about:

1. Do you know teens who have an obsession with going steady? Explain.
2. Is it hard to be friends when that person has a steady boy/girlfriend?
3. What do you think about the teens you know who go steady? Is it a winner/bummer/or somewhere in between?

# *Feeling Like Two Cents*

Inferiority has to be included in the top five problems people face. All ages are affected. Too often that problem bugs a person all his life. He compares himself with others and ends up feeling like two cents—or less.

We spend hours sulking, grumping and drooling over what we don't have but wish we did. Because we feel inferior, we are prone to envy or jealousy. Those attitudes are so hideous that we hate to admit we have them, but we do. Probably most of us are affected, more or less.

Envy gives us heartburn. It makes us uncomfortable and keeps us at war with ourselves. We are never at peace because we are disappointed with what we have and who we are. In severe cases it bothers us every day.

Jealousy is called the green monster. Few things drain the fun out of a friendship faster than jealousy. We wish we had their clothes, their home, their talent, their looks, and on and on. What are we saying? We believe our friend is better than we are. We feel like two cents around him because we are jealous.

It's hard to keep a healthy relationship when one of the friends feels inferior to the other. They can't give and take equally. There is a continual attitude that he can and I can't; he has and I don't.

Having these feelings of not measuring up explains why some have trouble keeping friends for very long. Since one person feels inferior, the relationship is always strained. The friendship simply isn't equal. After living under that load for a few months or years, the weight becomes too much. The jealous person pulls himself away and looks for another friend. However, that second friendship probably will not last, either. The same problem will happen over and over again until that person can control his envy.

He is unlikely to handle his envy because he doesn't recognize it. Consequently he bounces from friend to friend.

Inside he hurts. He can't come to peace with himself. He needs to understand the mercy and peace that Jesus Christ offers. He needs to talk to someone who can discuss his value system and listen to what some of his fears might be. God reassures us of our equality and worth.

Many of us have left great friends behind because we kept comparing ourselves and thought we came up short. We all know it's dumb but that doesn't stop us. That monster called "envy" keeps making us miserable.

*"A heart at peace gives life to the body, but envy rots the bones"* (Prov. 14:30).

## Some things to think about:

1. Think of an example of greed that you have seen.
2. How do you keep envy in check?
3. What should you do when you find yourself wanting what a friend has?

# The Sex Battle!

There is no easy way to win the war called sex. The pressure is almost unbearable. Our bodies scream for attention. Movies praise sex as an entrance into adulthood. Young people act like everyone is involved in sexual promiscuity and insist you should, too. It's doubtful that most teenagers face any challenge tougher than this one.

Because of the sexual dilemma today, the older generation is happy to be past that period in their life. They wouldn't want to go through the sexual frustration of being single again for anything.

Having gone through the sexual revolution and seen the many pitfalls facing young people, parents, as well as everyone else, are ready to give advice on how to handle sex. I've probably done it a couple of times myself. Sometimes teenagers tire of advice and would appreciate a bit of understanding instead.

There are no special formulas to keep the big, bad demon of sex from your door. However, it might help to remember a few principles once in a while.

First, remember, the person who wants to have sex with you *cares little about your problems.* His main goal is his own satisfaction. If you get hurt, humiliated, confused or pregnant, it's your burden. Even if your partner means well, there isn't much he can do. Your troubles will remain your troubles.

Second, *don't trust your body.* Let your mind, not your glands, run your life. That's true in all of life. When your brain goes out to lunch, the rest of you is in trouble.

Third, *only you can draw the line.* How far is too far? How long is too long? How often is too often? In the final analysis no one but you can protect you. If you are careless, there are a zillion people who will take you too far. And some of these people appear to be the nicest Christians you have ever met. Read that sentence again.

After we go too far, we try to blame everyone else: My parents didn't tell me. The school class didn't explain it. My pastor never discussed it. But none of the excuses will help. The bottom line is: each of us must be responsible for our own actions—and we are.

Four, *God is pulling for you.* Jesus Christ does understand how hard it is. He was young, He was sexual, He was tempted in every way we are. God furnishes encouragement, inner strength and even warnings. He hopes you hold on and make it through this sexual maze.

No amount of information, education or scare tactics will stop a person from making a mistake unless he wants to stop. Pump up your *want to.* God will hang in there with you as you fight back and come out the winner. He has called you to be clean before Him, no matter what your age or temptation.

*"Even youths grow tired and weary, and young men stumble and fall; but those who hope in the Lord will renew their strength"* (Isa. 40:30, 31).

## Some things to think about:

1. How do you choose the movies you attend?
2. Name some good activities you can plan for dates.
3. If you feel you should drop a friend, how would you go about it?

# Embarrassed by Brothers and Sisters

Whenever someone introduced Ann, she would automatically say, "That's my name, but I'm not anything like my sister."

Ann's sister had a terrible and well-known reputation. Practically every day Ann felt self-conscious about her sister's actions. Sometimes she cried. Other days she was tough, held her head high and led her own life.

If we have a collection of siblings, we are sure to be affected by their behavior. They might succeed so well in school that we hate to follow them. It's also possible that they have muddied the waters so badly that you hate to admit you belong to the family.

How many times have we cringed when someone said, "Oh, you must be Linda's sister"?

Why can't we stand on our own qualities? Why do people have to compare us with other family members? There is probably no way to avoid the connection. We do live in a context, and our brothers and sisters help make up the mix. Sometimes it is an advantage to be related to someone. Other times it's practically a curse.

The Bible tells us about Joseph, who didn't get along with his brothers. Part of it was his fault, part was his brothers and more than a little was because of their father, Jacob. They hassled each other a great deal, and finally the brothers were fed up. When they got off alone with Joseph, they dumped him into a well and left him for dead.

Fortunately, Judah, one of the brothers, talked them into selling their sibling into slavery instead. He brought in twenty shekels of silver and was whisked off to Egypt.

While in Egypt Joseph rose to prime minister and later was able to help the brothers who sold him as a slave. He learned to love and forgive and help the relatives who had treated him miserably.

We all have tough times and often react poorly. Our brothers and sisters will go through periods when their behavior turns ugly. Those sour moods are bound to affect us both indirectly and directly. We may not be able to explain our siblings' actions; they probably can't either. That is when we need to keep a few guidelines in mind.

1. The best reputation you have is your own behavior. Everyone who knows you will see what your character is like. No sibling can confuse your friends about you.

2. Never try to match your brother or sister for good or bad. We make terrible imitations but great originals.

3. It doesn't usually help to try to change someone else. They must see the need to change. The best we can do is control the way we react.

4. Teasing is part of life. It sometimes hurts, but don't make it worse by taking it too seriously.

5. Respond to brothers and sisters with love. Dumping them in wells is impractical and illegal.

6. Ask Jesus Christ to help us mellow. He can give us a better perspective. Love and forgiveness are sometimes tough to come by but are the heart of a sane life.

*"Then he threw his arms around his brother Benjamin and wept, and Benjamin embraced him, weeping. And he kissed all his brothers and wept over them. Afterward his brothers talked with him"* (Gen. 45:14, 15).

## Some things to think about:

1. Name two kind things Joseph did.
2. How can you tell your brother that he teases too much?
3. Do you think forgiving someone helps him change? How?

# How to Dump a Friend

What do you do when it's time to split with a friend? Especially if that friend is of a different gender. And you happen to like that opposite gendered friend.

If you can keep a cool head (and most people can't), you can learn a few simple, direct steps which will let that friend down as easily as possible.

Special note: There is no way to guarantee how your friend will react. The best you can do is try to control how *you* will act. Your self-control is the key to kindness.

*Step one:* Be sure of your self.

Is this really what you want? If not, is this something you must do anyway? Maybe the situation has deteriorated to the point where you dare not continue. Make peace with yourself about the decision. If you try to cut it off but you are uncertain, anything might happen.

*Step two:* Be kind.

You aren't going to slay the person. Don't be unnecessarily harsh or cruel. Use the best terms possible and even throw in a compliment or two. The person does have a few good qualities and is entitled to them.

*Step three:* Be firm.

If your mind is made up, sound like it. By hesitating and stammering, you send mixed signals. If your friend hears two different tones, he will grab the one he wants. That isn't fair if your decision has really been made.

*Step four:* Wish that friend well.

When necessary, forgive the person for whatever he may have done. The shortest route to peace is to forgive someone who has hurt you. Tell your friend you hope he wins the sweepstakes and that the prize of Crackle Crisps is something he can use. Be sincere about it. Bitterness never helps.

*Step five:* You make up this one. Every individual is different and each personality his own. Add to this list a touch that you consider important. When good people look for a good way to get things done, they come up with some gems.

The key to saying "so long" to a friend is found in what Jesus Christ said. He taught us to do unto others as we would have others treat us (Luke 6:31). If you were about to be dumped, how would you like it done? That question will lead us to act kindly almost every time.

## Some things to think about:

1. If your friend were going to dump someone of the opposite gender, what advice would you give?
2. If your friend were slicing off a friendship with someone of the same gender, what advice would you give?
3. If the person refuses to accept being dumped, what do you do?

# A Hard Word to Use

Have you ever wanted to say "I love you" but couldn't? You really felt it from the bottom of your toes and wanted to express it, but the words choked in your throat.

It's a common experience. We find it hard to express how we feel. Sometimes we aren't sure we trust our feelings. At other times we aren't sure if we understand the words.

Part of the reason we have trouble with the word "love" is that we have assigned a sexual connotation to it. If we use the word, will it be misunderstood? Does it say more than we want? We are wise to use it cautiously, but it would be too bad if we failed to use it at all.

Teenagers usually love their parents. They would even like to tell them so. The problem is that they are afraid it sounds "corny" and aren't really sure what the word means anyway. Should they use the same word with their father that they would like to use with a boyfriend? That seems abnormal. They want to express their emotions, but they feel awkward even trying.

Because we are uncomfortable with the word, we rationalize reasons not to use it. After all, don't parents know that you love them? Don't you show it in other ways? Maybe you do. But nothing takes the place of the magic words. Words are not enough but words are essential. None of us dares to take love for granted. We can't leave parents guessing.

If it's difficult to say, maybe we need to ease into it. Why not a short note? Thank them for what they did and then write out the words, "I love you." After you write it out on a few notes, it will become easier to say.

A second step is talking on the run. We all do it. As we hustle past the living room, we toss out a few words like, "The car's out of gas." Or "Sorry about the dent." Or "I flunked geometry." We blurt it out and keep moving because we aren't prepared to discuss it.

Give "I love you" a few quick blurts. "Thanks for the car. By the way, I love you," and you are gone like a flea.

None of this sounds like much, but it's a start. It's all a buildup to that one special moment when you will look a parent in the eye and say, "I love you."

We have a great example in God talking to His Son. In direct, unequivocal terms, God wanted His Son to know exactly how He felt. The best way was to tell Him. That way Jesus didn't have to guess.

*"And a voice came from heaven: 'You are my Son, whom I love; with you I am well pleased' "* (Luke 3:22).

## Some things to think about:

1. Does your family find it easy to express love to each other? How do you usually do it?
2. How can one improve his ability to show love?
3. Is there a person to whom you find it easy to say "I love you"?

# Friends in
# High Places

Connie was the kind of person who genuinely enjoyed people. She liked to do things in groups. Her idea of fun was working on the yearbook, squirting water at car washes and laughing out loud at the local pizza parlor. Connie was bright. That meant she was alert and sharp, living on the happy edge of life.

But sometimes Connie was alone and quiet. Fortunately she had learned to appreciate being by herself. She had her room to take care of, her nails to mess with and letters to write.

Being alone also helped Connie get in touch with her special friend. She knew she had a friend in high places. Connie had learned the pleasure of visiting with one extraordinary friend. She called Him God, Father, Friend, and often felt close to Him. Those were the times she liked the best.

If she stopped to think about it, her conversations with her friend were actually prayers. But she seldom stopped to think about it. It was more like sharing—the way we talk to someone we have known for years. They had "chats."

Connie's talks weren't one-sided, either. She would read a few Bible verses to let God speak to her. Sometimes she sat silently and felt her mood change. Connie was at peace—confident and secure. She accepted that as part of God talking to her.

There are many ways to think of God. Connie was aware that God was a judge, counselor, creator and a shipload more. But most of the time she zeroed in on one thought. God was her friend. And they had a close relationship. God was with her at the football game; He was there when she decorated floats. But He felt especially near when Connie spent a few minutes alone.

Teenagers need a few good friends. Connie was fortunate to grab a rich relationship with someone in high places.

*"My Father, my friend from my youth"* (Jer. 3:4).

## Some things to think about:

1. How do you like to visit with God?
2. List some guidelines for staying in touch with God.
3. When do you make time for prayer?

# Cruising with Your Parents

The first time I saw teenagers cruising was in Sterling, Kansas. We had moved to the area that day and were looking for a place to eat. As we drove into town, we saw a dozen cars cruising back and forth on Main Street. When the kids in each car met the others, they beeped their horns. We didn't know if it was a car rodeo or the start of a new religion.

Years later, when our children were teenagers, the ritual was still alive in Nebraska. An exciting evening consisted of "cruising the square." Cars would practically get in line to spend the evening making left-hand turns and beeping at friends.

I never understood the dance of the cars, but it seemed to make the teenagers happy. One evening I decided to jump into their world and find out what it was all about.

Driving home from Grand Island, Jim was in the front seat; Mary and June were in the back. Their mother wasn't along. Suddenly I said, "I've got a great idea. Why don't we go cruising?"

With that terse announcement I turned left at the square and joined the parade of the simple. Immediately I started honking my horn at the cars we met and waving at the other drivers.

Jim caught on to the problem instantly. "I ain't cruising with my dad," he growled. He sank like a rock. Squirreling down into the front seat, he disappeared.

Responding quickly, Mary and June folded up like flaps on an old box.

Suddenly I was cruising all by myself. But I couldn't let that discourage me. I continued driving, honking and waving.

"Hi, Mike. What's happening, Al?" I knew them all and had a blast. I can see now why teenagers like to cruise. Too bad I had to do it alone.

My wife Pat got in on the action later. Everyone was talking about a new movie that was out. It was one of those "teenagers are growing into adulthood" things that are usually gross. Just talking, I dared Jim to take his mother to see it. He asked her and to everyone's amazement she accepted.

They spent the evening sitting in a theater, a teenage boy and his mom, watching a movie that would embarrass a sailor. After that Pat stuck with "Little House on the Prairie."

It's fun to visit the world of teenagers, but parents can't stay there. Young people need to enjoy their sphere and adults should be grateful for theirs. Each of us becomes clumsy trying to live in the other's world.

Be young. Have a great time. Adults are too busy enjoying their life to stay very long in yours.

*"Be happy, young man, while you are young, and let your heart give you joy in the days of your youth"* (Eccles. 11:9).

## Some things to think about:

1. Have you participated in one of your parent's activities that totally bored you? Explain.
2. Have your parents gone to one of your activities and you wished they weren't there? Tell about it.

# Importance on Looks

Recently I was in an airport where practically every schedule was off. Planes were two hours late; lines were long; computers kept shutting down; one airline had five hundred claims for lost luggage that day.

It was amazing to watch people under stress. That day, in another city, a ticket agent was attacked and beaten by a frustrated passenger. The passenger was arrested. Ticket agents quit their jobs and walked away.

People who looked cool, well-groomed and prosperous sometimes blew their cork and became abusive. Others who were shaggy haired, overweight, even dumpy looking remained pleasant and cheerful. One lady, twisted into a wheelchair, kept her contented smile and took life as it came.

In all these situations, a person's physical appearance had little to do with his behavior under pressure. Some looked like the inside of a teenager's locker, but they were great to be around.

Most of us are hung up on how people look. That's why some say, "Clothes make the person." Some also think expensive cars make people. It's a weird value system.

We all know better in our heads, but we still envy the people who look as if they walked out of a jean's commercial. And we miss knowing some terrific friends because they look like last week's laundry.

I had a friend who dressed in the latest fashions the thrift shop had to offer. He put together old cheap clothes; his pants went out of style with Eisenhower. My guess is he combed his hair with his fingers.

Normally people did not pick out Jerry and try to talk with him. But those few who made the effort met a smart guy with a great sense of humor. They found a caring friend who was quick to help others.

It's a lousy game and most people know it. We let a hairstyle stop us from getting to understand someone. We allow a brand of tennis shoes to tell us whether a person is any good or not. With Christians it should be different—though too often it isn't. We're attracted to the popular, the wealthy, the athletic, the leaders—partly because we want to be like them. The fact is, God wants us to accept *all* kinds of people.

Some people couldn't stand Jesus Christ because of His "poor" selection of friends. He collected the unpopular. He spent time with the beggars, handicapped, sick, blind and even became friends with the dreaded tax collectors and hookers. Jesus refused to judge people by their designer tunics or their Italian sandals.

Many Christian young people agree with Him. They get to know others, no matter what their "social status." Caringly they share their Christian faith. They get to know many kinds of people and include them in what they do.

*"Some men came carrying a paralytic on a mat and tried to take him into the house to lay him before Jesus. When they could not find a way to do this because of the crowd, they went up on the roof and lowered him on his mat through the tiles into the middle of the crowd, right in front of Jesus. When Jesus saw their faith, he said, 'Friend, your sins are forgiven' "* (Luke 5:18–20).

## Some things to think about:

1. Do you have friends of another race or economic level than your own?
2. Are there cliques in your school? Explain.
3. Are there cliques in your church? Explain.

# Why Do They Drink?

Almost all teenagers drink alcohol because of their friends.

Drinking is a people problem, not a substance problem. Seldom does anyone get into trouble because he was too thirsty. The overwhelming majority drink because they feel a pressure from the friends they hang around with.

It's almost too simple to accept, but if you discuss it with other young people, you'll find they drink because they believe (or know) that their peers expect them to drink. That's the problem in a nutshell.

We crash cars, get arrested, get pregnant, lose our jobs, fight our parents continually, are confronted by the police, mess up our careers because we think our friends expect us to drink.

If we talk to a group of young people, it's nearly impossible to find one who will say, "I really enjoy the taste of suds." If you ask them to list eight reasons why teenagers drink, the word taste will almost never appear on the page. Their favorite beverage is probably something as calm as hot chocolate. But taste and thirst are not the issue. Pleasing friends and trying to make new friends is the issue.

Many teenagers would like to give up alcohol, but they don't want to be the first one to say no. Since no one is willing to be first, it hardly ever happens. They all go along because no one wants to be left out. What they may not know is that if a few teenagers would begin saying no, soon many would say the same thing.

To be perfectly honest, the Bible says some flattering things about wine. King David praised God for giving the good gift of wine to His creation (Ps. 104:15). However, God didn't create wine so David could wrap his chariot around a tree, beat his bride, or set fire to the hay fields. People are too adept at letting alcohol make a fool out of them.

The Bible is careful to spell out the harmful power in alcohol. It explains that "wine is a mocker and beer a brawler" (Prov. 20:1). Alcohol will make a fool out of us. It will reduce our ability to think, cut our reflexes down to slow motion, double our vision and turn our stomachs into geysers going off every fifteen minutes.

Many teenagers in our community have died because of alcohol. Sooner or later most of us will have a friend who is killed because of alcohol abuse.

Friends cause friends to abuse alcohol. Friends die because friends cause friends to abuse alcohol.

## Some things to think about:

1. How prevalent is drinking in your high school?
2. Does your community have a program to discourage drinking?
3. What should your attitude be if your friends abuse alcohol?